Pearson
PUBLISHING

Student Handbook

Key Skills:
Information Technology
Level 3

Gareth Williams

Cartoons by Steve Clarke

Name: ....

Class: ....

School: ....

....

Exam board: ....

Specification number: ....

Candidate number: ....

Centre number: ....

Further copies of this publication may be obtained from:

Pearson Publishing
Chesterton Mill, French's Road, Cambridge CB4 3NP
Tel 01223 350555 Fax 01223 356484

Email info@pearson.co.uk
Web site www.pearsonpublishing.co.uk

ISBN: 1 85749 703 1

Published by Pearson Publishing 2002
© Pearson Publishing 2002

Contents

Introduction

Everyone's experience of education is different. However, there are a number of valuable skills that underpin our education. These should help us through all areas of our education and future learning in college, at university, at work or in our own time.

What are the Key Skills?

Key Skills are:

- **general skills** – they are used to improve your learning and performance. They are needed in education, work and everyday life
- **essential in education** because they help you to demonstrate and communicate your ideas and knowledge
- **essential in employment** – if you have Key Skills certificates, an employer will feel confident about your ability in specific areas, eg IT. Most people will have several jobs during their lifetime. Key Skills are essential to help you to adapt to different types of job and to remain employable during your working life
- **essential in everyday life** because they are the skills you will need repeatedly.

The Key Skills qualification was made available from September 2000 and is designed to allow students to demonstrate and improve their proficiency in up to six different areas. The three main Key Skills are:

- Communication
- Application of Number
- Information Technology.

Together these make up the Key Skills qualification. The three wider Key Skills are:

- Working with Others
- Improving own Learning and Performance
- Problem Solving.

The first three Key Skills are available at different levels (1 to 5) with each level representing a progression from one to the next. The last three Key Skills are available from Levels 1 to 3.

Key Skills may be obtained from NVQs, GNVQs, GCE AS/A-Levels or the International Baccalaureate. This handbook is concerned with the Information Technology Key Skill at Level 3.

The Key Skill IT course is designed to increase your skills and knowledge of using computer software programs. It will also increase your effectiveness in school, college and business by developing your competence in solving problems using the wide range of tools offered by IT.

Obtaining your certificates

In order to secure this qualification, you will need to provide evidence, either through specially designated tasks, or through tasks in courses you are already studying. This evidence should then be collected together in a clearly indexed portfolio.

There will be an internal assessment of your portfolio. It will be assessed by your teachers and verified (checked) by the examination board. When your portfolio material reaches a satisfactory standard, it will be signed off by the standards moderator (external examiner) and you will receive a Unit Certificate.

You will also need to pass an externally-verified examination, lasting 90 minutes. This is called an External Assessment Instrument (EAI). The exam will consist of questions equivalent to Level 7 of the National Curriculum (ie about Grade C GCSE). When you pass an EAI, you receive a Test Certificate.

'Your assignment, should you choose to accept it...'

Using this handbook

This handbook is presented via four main parts:

- *Part 1* explains Information Technology and how you need to apply your IT skills.

- *Part 2* explains what is needed for your portfolio in order to obtain your Unit Certificate. It offers a sample assignment to show you how a portfolio can be put together to meet the necessary criteria.

- *Part 3* of this handbook focuses on skills in the different software programs. The skills required are more advanced than those you may have covered at Key Stages 3 and 4 (up to Year 11). For example, how to perform a mailmerge in Microsoft® Word or an IF statement in Microsoft® Excel. The detailed procedures are based on the programs available in Microsoft® Office 2000. These may vary slightly if you are using other versions of Microsoft® Office.

- *Part 4* offers an example examination paper together with guidance and instructions on answering the questions.

In addition, there is a glossary of terms on pages 116 to 118 and a list of useful Web sites on pages 119 and 120.

The tracking calendars, assignment checklist and the outline project are differentiated from the rest of the text by the use of a background tint.

The tracking calendars and forms can be downloaded from the Pearson Publishing Web site at http://www.pearsonpublishing.co.uk/publications/extras/, if you wish to use them in your portfolio. Some databases (see pages 51 and 100) are also provided on this site.

Part 1

The skills

Key Skills: Information Technology

What is this unit about?

This unit is about applying your IT skills to suit different purposes.

You will need to show that you can:

- plan and use different sources to search for and select information

- explore, develop and exchange information, and derive new information

- present information, including text, numbers and images.

What you need to know

The following notes tell you what you need to learn and practise to feel confident about applying IT skills in your studies, work or other aspects of your life.

In **planning and selecting information**, you need to know how to:

- plan a substantial activity by breaking it down into a series of tasks

- compare the advantages and limitations of different sources of information (eg databases, the Internet, material to be scanned, files on disk, CD-ROMs) and select those suitable for your purpose (eg to obtain views of others, to produce financial data, product information or a multimedia presentation)

- choose appropriate techniques for finding information (eg database query techniques, Internet search engines, multiple criteria including relational operators such as less than/greater than, and logical criteria such as AND/OR/NOT conditions) and use them to carry out effective searches

- make selections based on relevance to your purpose and judgements on quality (eg your own and others' views on accuracy and reliability of content).

In **developing information**, you need to know how to:

- enter and bring together information in a consistent form (eg lists, tables, frames, types of images) and use automated routines (eg macros, icons, database query and report routines, validation for database entries)

- create and use structures and procedures for developing text, images and numbers (eg sort and group information, use mailmerge, analyse and interpret numerical data using spreadsheet software, generate graphs and charts)

- explore information (eg design and develop lines of enquiry, change values and rules in a model to make predictions and test hypotheses)

- derive new information (eg evaluate information from different sources to reach and justify a conclusion, use facilities to calculate or deduce results)

- use methods of exchanging information to support your purpose (eg email, shared access to documents, collaborative development of information).

In **presenting information**, you need to know how to:

- develop the structure of your presentation (eg modify templates and paragraph styles, apply automatic referencing facilities such as page numbers, dates and file names), and use the views of others to guide refinements (eg obtain feedback on content, layout, format, style)

- develop and refine the presentation of text, images and numbers (eg improve impact by changing format or layout, combine information, overlay images on text)

- present information so that it meets your purpose and the needs of the audience (eg compare paper-based, single form, mixed form and multimedia presentations and choose the most suitable one available)

- ensure work is accurate and makes sense (eg proofread, use a spellchecker, seek the views of others).

You will also need to know:

- the implications of using IT, comparing your use of IT with systems used elsewhere
- when it is necessary to observe copyright or confidentiality
- how to save your work for easy retrieval, for managing versions and to avoid loss
- how to identify errors and their causes and minimise risks from viruses
- how to work safely and minimise health risks.

What you must do

The following notes describe the skills you must show. All your work for this section will be assessed. You must have evidence that you can do all the things listed on pages 2, 3 and above.

You must plan and carry through at least one substantial activity that includes tasks for IT3.1, IT3.2 and IT3.3 – these are explained below. They are the criteria which will be referred to throughout this handbook. For example:

| This means Information Technology | This means Level 3 | This means the first section of your work, ie *Planning the activity and interpreting information*. |

IT3.1 – Plan and use different sources to search for, and select, information required for **two** different purposes.

Evidence must show you can:

- *plan how to obtain and use the information required to meet the purpose of your activity*
- *choose appropriate sources and techniques for finding information and carry out effective searches*
- *make selections based on judgements of relevance and quality.*

4

IT3.2 – Explore, develop, and exchange information, and derive new information, to meet **two** different purposes.

- *enter and bring together information in a consistent form, using automated routines where appropriate*
- *create and use appropriate structures and procedures to explore and develop information and derive new information*
- *use effective methods of exchanging information to support your purpose*

IT3.3 – Present information from different sources for **two** different purposes and audiences.

Your work must include at least **one** example of text, **one** example of images and **one** example of numbers.

- *develop the structure and content of your presentation using the views of others, where appropriate, to guide refinements*
- *present information effectively, using a format and style that suits your purpose and audience*
- *ensure your work is accurate and makes sense.*

The assignment checklist on pages 17 and 18 can be used to check that you have covered all of the tasks for IT3.1, IT3.2 and IT3.3.

Guidance

This section describes some of the activities you might like to use to develop and show your IT skills. It also contains examples of the sort of evidence you could produce to prove you have the skills required.

*'The evidence is in there **somewhere**...'*

You will have opportunities to develop and apply your IT skills during your work, studies or other activities. For example, when:

- planning, carrying out and reporting findings from an investigation or project
- designing and presenting a product
- researching information and reporting outcomes to customers or clients
- exchanging information and ideas with work colleagues or other students.

You will need time to practise your skills and prepare for assessment. So it is important to plan ahead. For example, to identify an activity that is substantial enough to provide opportunities for following through tasks for IT3.1, IT3.2 and IT3.3. You may need to do additional tasks to cover all the requirements of Part B.

The purpose for using IT can be decided by you or by other people, but you must make sure that the work you produce suits this purpose. Using IT can contribute evidence of your use of other Key Skills, such as Communication and Application of Number.

You will need to think about the quality of your IT skills and check that your evidence covers all the criteria requirements.

Examples of evidence include the following:

IT3.1 Plan and select information:

- A description of the substantial activity and tasks. A plan for obtaining and using the information required.

- Printouts of the relevant information with notes of sources compared and used. Notes on how you made searches and selected information.

IT3.2 Develop information:

- Printouts, with notes, or a record from an assessor who observed your use of IT, showing how you have exchanged, explored and developed information and derived new information.

- Notes of automated routines.

IT3.3 Present information:

- Working drafts, or a record from an assessor who observed your screen displays, showing how you developed the presentation using information from different sources.

- Printouts or a static or dynamic screen display of your final work, including examples of text, images and numbers.

- If producing certain types of evidence creates difficulties, due to disability or other factors, you may be able to use other ways to show your achievement. Ask your tutor or supervisor for further information.

Part 2

Your portfolio

Planning your approach

Many post-16 courses are divided into two sections. For example, you can study an AS-level in Year 12 and then the A-level in Year 13. It is advisable to try and complete most of your Key Skills work in Year 12 as this will allow you more time to concentrate on A-levels in Year 13. It is therefore a good idea to begin collecting evidence for your Key Skills portfolio as soon as possible in Year 12. It may also help you to adjust to the new demands of post-16 courses as you will need to focus on skills that will be very useful to help you through your main courses.

The externally-assessed Key Skills IT examination can be taken at a number of points throughout the year and can be retaken as many times as necessary. You will need to discuss the best time for you to take the exam with your assessor.

If you are confident that you have mastered the skills to the required level then you will benefit from taking the exam at the earliest opportunity. You should also be able to gather the required evidence fairly quickly. This will then allow you to concentrate on your core studies. If you need time to develop the skills then you will evidently benefit from delaying taking the exam until you have been able to practise them.

Tracking calendars

It is important to keep a clear record of your Key Skills progress. The tracking calendars on pages 12 to 14 allow you to keep a record of the assignments for each element of the IT Key Skill, as well as any exam preparation you may wish to do.

To use the tracking calendars, choose a different colour for each of the headings in the key below and fill in the boxes beside them. (If you wish to record other dates or deadlines, etc, you can add them to the key in the spaces provided.) Use the key to colour in the relevant sections of the appropriate tracking calendar. You will then be able to see at a glance when you have to complete your Key Skills work.

Key

Assignment deadlines	☐
Exam preparation	☐
Mock exam dates	☐
Dates of exam	☐
....	☐
....	☐
....	☐
....	☐

Tracking calendar 2001-2002

Month	S	S	M	T	W	T	F	S	S	M	T	W	T	F	S	S	M	T	W	T	F	S	S	M	T	W	T	F	S	S	M	T	W	T	F	S	S
SEP	1	2	3	4	5	6	7	8	9	10	11	12	13	14	15	16	17	18	19	20	21	22	23	24	25	26	27	28	29	30							
OCT			1	2	3	4	5	6	7	8	9	10	11	12	13	14	15	16	17	18	19	20	21	22	23	24	25	26	27	28	29	30	31				
NOV						1	2	3	4	5	6	7	8	9	10	11	12	13	14	15	16	17	18	19	20	21	22	23	24	25	26	27	28	29	30		
DEC	1	2	3	4	5	6	7	8	9	10	11	12	13	14	15	16	17	18	19	20	21	22	23	24	25	26	27	28	29	30	31						
JAN				1	2	3	4	5	6	7	8	9	10	11	12	13	14	15	16	17	18	19	20	21	22	23	24	25	26	27	28	29	30	31			
FEB							1	2	3	4	5	6	7	8	9	10	11	12	13	14	15	16	17	18	19	20	21	22	23	24	25	26	27	28			
MAR							1	2	3	4	5	6	7	8	9	10	11	12	13	14	15	16	17	18	19	20	21	22	23	24	25	26	27	28	29	30	31
APR			1	2	3	4	5	6	7	8	9	10	11	12	13	14	15	16	17	18	19	20	21	22	23	24	25	26	27	28	29	30					
MAY					1	2	3	4	5	6	7	8	9	10	11	12	13	14	15	16	17	18	19	20	21	22	23	24	25	26	27	28	29	30	31		
JUN	1	2	3	4	5	6	7	8	9	10	11	12	13	14	15	16	17	18	19	20	21	22	23	24	25	26	27	28	29	30							
JUL			1	2	3	4	5	6	7	8	9	10	11	12	13	14	15	16	17	18	19	20	21	22	23	24	25	26	27	28	29	30	31				
AUG						1	2	3	4	5	6	7	8	9	10	11	12	13	14	15	16	17	18	19	20	21	22	23	24	25	26	27	28	29	30	31	

Tracking calendar 2002-2003

	S	S	M	T	W	T	F	S	S	M	T	W	T	F	S	S	M	T	W	T	F	S	S	M	T	W	T	F	S	S	M	T	W	T	F	S	S
SEP		1	2	3	4	5	6	7	8	9	10	11	12	13	14	15	16	17	18	19	20	21	22	23	24	25	26	27	28	29	30						
OCT			1	2	3	4	5	6	7	8	9	10	11	12	13	14	15	16	17	18	19	20	21	22	23	24	25	26	27	28	29	30	31				
NOV				1	2	3	4	5	6	7	8	9	10	11	12	13	14	15	16	17	18	19	20	21	22	23	24	25	26	27	28	29	30				
DEC		1	2	3	4	5	6	7	8	9	10	11	12	13	14	15	16	17	18	19	20	21	22	23	24	25	26	27	28	29	30	31					
JAN			1	2	3	4	5	6	7	8	9	10	11	12	13	14	15	16	17	18	19	20	21	22	23	24	25	26	27	28	29	30	31				
FEB	1	2	3	4	5	6	7	8	9	10	11	12	13	14	15	16	17	18	19	20	21	22	23	24	25	26	27	28									
MAR	1	2	3	4	5	6	7	8	9	10	11	12	13	14	15	16	17	18	19	20	21	22	23	24	25	26	27	28	29	30	31						
APR			1	2	3	4	5	6	7	8	9	10	11	12	13	14	15	16	17	18	19	20	21	22	23	24	25	26	27	28	29	30					
MAY				1	2	3	4	5	6	7	8	9	10	11	12	13	14	15	16	17	18	19	20	21	22	23	24	25	26	27	28	29	30	31			
JUN		1	2	3	4	5	6	7	8	9	10	11	12	13	14	15	16	17	18	19	20	21	22	23	24	25	26	27	28	29	30						
JUL			1	2	3	4	5	6	7	8	9	10	11	12	13	14	15	16	17	18	19	20	21	22	23	24	25	26	27	28	29	30	31				
AUG				1	2	3	4	5	6	7	8	9	10	11	12	13	14	15	16	17	18	19	20	21	22	23	24	25	26	27	28	29	30	31			

Tracking calendar 2003-2004

	S	S	M	T	W	T	F	S	S	M	T	W	T	F	S	S	M	T	W	T	F	S	S	M	T	W	T	F	S	S	M	T	W	T	F	S	S
SEP			1	2	3	4	5	6	7	8	9	10	11	12	13	14	15	16	17	18	19	20	21	22	23	24	25	26	27	28	29	30					
OCT					1	2	3	4	5	6	7	8	9	10	11	12	13	14	15	16	17	18	19	20	21	22	23	24	25	26	27	28	29	30	31		
NOV	1	2	3	4	5	6	7	8	9	10	11	12	13	14	15	16	17	18	19	20	21	22	23	24	25	26	27	28	29	30							
DEC			1	2	3	4	5	6	7	8	9	10	11	12	13	14	15	16	17	18	19	20	21	22	23	24	25	26	27	28	29	30	31				
JAN						1	2	3	4	5	6	7	8	9	10	11	12	13	14	15	16	17	18	19	20	21	22	23	24	25	26	27	28	29	30	31	
FEB		1	2	3	4	5	6	7	8	9	10	11	12	13	14	15	16	17	18	19	20	21	22	23	24	25	26	27	28	29							
MAR			1	2	3	4	5	6	7	8	9	10	11	12	13	14	15	16	17	18	19	20	21	22	23	24	25	26	27	28	29	30	31				
APR						1	2	3	4	5	6	7	8	9	10	11	12	13	14	15	16	17	18	19	20	21	22	23	24	25	26	27	28	29	30		
MAY	1	2	3	4	5	6	7	8	9	10	11	12	13	14	15	16	17	18	19	20	21	22	23	24	25	26	27	28	29	30	31						
JUN				1	2	3	4	5	6	7	8	9	10	11	12	13	14	15	16	17	18	19	20	21	22	23	24	25	26	27	28	29	30				
JUL						1	2	3	4	5	6	7	8	9	10	11	12	13	14	15	16	17	18	19	20	21	22	23	24	25	26	27	28	29	30	31	
AUG		1	2	3	4	5	6	7	8	9	10	11	12	13	14	15	16	17	18	19	20	21	22	23	24	25	26	27	28	29	30	31					

Planning your portfolio material

There are two parts to the assessment of your Key Skills qualification: your portfolio of work and the examination. The form of the examination and an example paper are covered in *Part 4* of this handbook. In this part we will look at the requirements for the portfolio.

What is a portfolio?

A portfolio is a collection of your work that has been organised into a file or folder. This work provides the evidence that you are able to carry out all of the requirements outlined in the Key Skills syllabus successfully. Your portfolio should also contain a record showing the progress of your work. It should contain details of how work in your portfolio meets the syllabus criteria, how the file or folder is organised,  who has assessed the pieces of work and the dates of assessment. Your finished portfolio work will be assessed by your teachers. The examination board will ask for a sample of marked portfolio folders to be sent to the board so that standards can be checked in different schools across the country.

Activity ideas

The work contained in your portfolio must meet all the criteria set out in the specification and involve at least one 'substantial activity'. This substantial activity can come from your work in other subjects. For example, a History assignment, a Geography project, Business Studies coursework or a Science investigation. It could come from work experience, a community project or any area of your life of study, employment or leisure. Whatever you choose, it is necessary to cover all of the requirements listed in Part B of the specification as shown in the assignment checklist on pages 17 and 18. The type of software package(s) that you use to implement your activity can have an effect on producing the required evidence. For example, using a database package like

Microsoft® Access makes the evidence section *'enter and bring together information in a consistent form, using automated routines where appropriate'* quite straightforward by using queries and macros.

The formulae and functions of a spreadsheet, however, make the evidence section *'create and use appropriate structures and procedures to explore and develop information and derive new information'* quite easy to achieve.

Whatever ideas you have for the portfolio activity, it is important that you can produce all the evidence required for each of the three sections, as outlined on pages 2 to 7.

Note that some of the work and evidence presented in your IT portfolio will meet the requirements for the Communication and Application of Number Key Skill modules.

In the sample assignment that follows on pages 19 to 29, where a topic covers one of the nine areas of evidence required by the specification, this has been indicated on the right-hand side by the use of circled letters. These refer to the assignment checklist (see pages 17 and 18) and hence you can see which of the criteria have been covered. A completed assignment checklist for the sample assignment is provided on pages 30 and 31.

Assignment checklist

Candidate's name:	
Title:	
Portfolio reference/page number:	Centre:
Assignment 1:	
Assignment 2:	

Every box in one column must have an entry tick (or page reference) to show it has been done.

	Assignment 1	Assignment 2	Teacher's initials

IT3.1 Plan and select information

A Plan and use different sources to search for, and select, information required for **two** different purposes ☐ ☐ ☐

　A₁ My first purpose:................................ ☐ ☐ ☐
　...
　...

　A₂ My second purpose:.............................. ☐ ☐ ☐
　...
　...

B Plan how to obtain and use the information required to meet the purpose of your activity ☐ ☐ ☐

C Choose appropriate sources and techniques for finding information and carry out effective searches ☐ ☐ ☐

D Make selections based on judgements of relevance and quality ☐ ☐ ☐

IT3.2 Develop information

E Explore, develop and exchange information, and derive new information, to meet **two** different purposes ☐ ☐ ☐

　E₁ My first purpose:................................. ☐ ☐ ☐
　...
　...

　E₂ My second purpose:.............................. ☐ ☐ ☐
　...
　...

		Assignment 1 2	Teacher's initials

F Enter and bring together information in a consistent form, using automated routines where appropriate ☐ ☐ ▢

G Create and use appropriate structures and procedures to explore and develop information and derive new information ☐ ☐ ▢

H Use effective methods of exchanging information to support your purpose ☐ ☐ ▢

IT3.3 Present information

I Present information from different sources for **two** different purposes and audiences ☐ ☐ ▢

I₁ My first purpose and audience:................. ☐ ☐ ▢
....
....
....

I₂ My second purpose and audience:........... ☐ ☐ ▢
....
....
....

J Develop the structure and content of your presentation using the views of others, where appropriate, to guide refinements ☐ ☐ ▢

K Present information effectively, using a format and style that suits your purpose and audience ☐ ☐ ▢

L Ensure your work is accurate and makes sense ☐ ☐ ▢

M Include at least one example using text ☐ ☐ ▢

N Include at least one example using images ☐ ☐ ▢

O Include at least one example using numbers ☐ ☐ ▢

Confirmation that all aspects of Information Technology are complete:

Candidate's signature: Teacher's signature:

Date: Print name:

Sample assignment

Year 12 at school is when students celebrate their 17th birthday. They may start taking driving lessons, and, therefore, taking a driving test and owning a car may become a significant part of daily life. For this example of how a 'substantial activity' could be tackled, we shall pose the question:

'Given £5000, what car could I buy and what would be the running costs?'

This sum of money would not be enough to purchase a new car so it would need to be a used car. For the more expensive models of car, the used car would need to be older to still fit within our price bracket. Being older, however, could lead to higher servicing, repair costs and the need for an MOT test.

The type of car we might like to own will depend on many different factors. For example, the car's 'image' or the safety features available, such as air bags and ABS brakes. Some of the features will affect the running costs of the car. For example, the engine size would be a factor in determining the cost of insurance, the fuel consumption and the annual road tax.

The object of this activity is to:

- obtain a list of 'desirable' used cars for potential purchase by students
- determine, for each car, the typical 'year of manufacture', taking into account the limited money available to purchase the car

- calculate the running costs of each car
- present the results of your findings to your audience.

To start this project it is necessary to produce a list of suitable cars to study. These will tend to be the smaller cars in the different manufacturers' ranges. Information from the main dealers and producing a questionnaire to circulate to all the sixth form would be a good way of identifying a range of ten to 15 popular cars on which to base the study. (You can collaborate with other students in the collection of data to obtain a wider range of cars.) You could also collect some primary research data by doing a survey of the student car park.

The assignment checklist on pages 30 and 31 has been completed for this sample assignment to show how the criteria have been met.

Research and processing data

The questionnaire could be designed in Microsoft® Publisher or Word or using the database Pinpoint. More information could be gained if a sample of Year 13 students were included in the survey. Carefully worded questions could find:

- the desired makes and models of car
- whether different models are preferred by boys compared to girls
- those actually purchased
- the reliability of cars owned
- the best and worst features.

For students who already own cars, information on the cost they are paying for insurance can be used later in the activity to validate the data obtained from insurance quotations taken from the Internet.

When designing a questionnaire, avoid using questions that require lengthy text answers. Make use of tick or check boxes, use scale ranges (for example, on a range of 1 to 5 with 5 being 'Essential' and 1 being 'Not important', would you consider the following features...) and use yes/no answers. Decide exactly what data you require and how it will be used before sending the questionnaire out for completion. Entering this information into a database will allow you to make searches and present the results graphically.

Having established a shortlist of cars, you can determine how old each car will have to be to fit within the price of £5000. Surveying used car sales nationally will help to show whether prices at local used car centres are competitive.

From magazine sources such as *Auto Trader* and *Exchange and Mart* and from used car sites on the Internet, the prices for the cars can be entered into a spreadsheet. The illustration below shows the average price for a VW Polo 1.4.

	A	B	C	D	E	F
1	**VW Polo 1.4**					
2						
3	**1995**	**1996**	**1997**	**1998**	**1999**	**2000**
4	£3,700	£4,500	£4,495	£6,300	£7,500	£8,600
5	£3,495	£5,595	£5,495	£6,495	£7,195	£7,695
6	£3,925	£3,795	£5,950	£5,995	£7,750	£7,500
7		£5,700	£5,900	£5,500	£7,500	£8,100
8		£5,095	£5,495	£6,200		£7,825
9		£4,770	£6,100	£6,495		
10			£4,600			
11						
12	£3,707	£4,909	£5,434	£6,164	£7,486	£7,944
13						
14						
15			=average(C4:C10)			
16						
17						

The prices of the used cars are entered into a spreadsheet and the average is found using the spreadsheet function

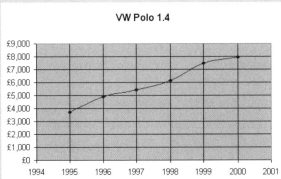

Using the spreadsheet to draw an XY (scatter) graph of the average prices shows how these change as the car gets older

Cars like the VW Polo hold their value well as they get older, hence the graph shows that a 1996 model is the most likely to be priced at £5000. A similar analysis for a Ford Fiesta shows that a newer 1998 model can be purchased as the car has a lower initial price.

In your project report, compare and comment on the different sources of information. State which were the most suitable, which were the easiest to use and which had the most relevant information for the purpose.

Running costs

In the next part of this activity, you should look at the annual running costs for each of the cars. The cost of running a car includes taking out insurance, paying the car tax, paying for fuel, the cost of servicing/repairs and the MOT test if the car is over three years old. You should also include the depreciation of the car over a year. This is the fall in value of the car as it gets older and an approximate figure can easily be calculated from the work above. In our example we shall look at Car 2 and assume 10 000 miles estimated annual mileage.

Fuel costs

Each car in our list is likely to have different figures for the fuel consumption in miles per gallon. This will depend on features such as the engine size and body design. The manufacturers' factsheets will often give several figures, one for driving around town (urban), one for longer distances using motorways and a combined value. It is important to ensure you use the same category for all your vehicles. These figures can generally also be found on the manufacturers' Web sites.

Example: Car 2 has a combined figure of 43.5 mpg (miles per gallon). To drive an average of 10 000 miles, the amount of fuel used is:

$$= \frac{10\ 000}{43.5} \text{ (gallons)}$$

Fuel at the pump is priced per litre; there are 4.5 litres in a gallon so the price per gallon is:

$$= \text{Pump price} \times 4.5$$

In a spreadsheet, we can combine these two calculations to show the cost of the fuel used during the year based on driving 10 000 miles as follows:

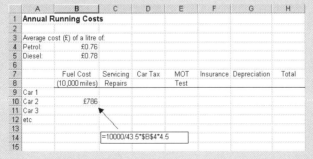

	A	B	C	D	E	F	G	H
1	**Annual Running Costs**							
2								
3	Average cost (£) of a litre of:							
4	Petrol:	£0.76						
5	Diesel:	£0.78						
6								
7		Fuel Cost	Servicing	Car Tax	MOT	Insurance	Depreciation	Total
8		(10,000 miles)	Repairs		Test			
9	Car 1							
10	Car 2	£786						
11	Car 3							
12	etc							
13								
14			=10000/43.5*$B$4*4.5					
15								

In the spreadsheet formula, the price of the fuel is obtained by referencing the cell B4. This allows the figures in the sheet to recalculate automatically if the price is changed. The dollar sign

'$' in front of the B and the 4 makes it an absolute cell reference (see page 70) and ensures the reference does not change as the cell formula is copied down for the other cars.

Servicing and repairs

Each manufacturer will advise on the interval between services. **B** **D** This will be based on a time interval or the number of miles the car has covered. The cost of repairs is more difficult to estimate; as the car becomes older, the cost of repairs is likely to rise.

Example: The manufacturer of Car 2 recommends a service every 12 months or 10 000 miles. The cost of this service is £150. As the car is nearly five years old, an estimate of £250 has been included for repair costs (eg replacing tyres, exhaust, etc).

Car tax

The annual car tax for used cars is determined by the size of the engine. (Note that for new cars, the tax is determined by engine emissions.)

Example: Car 2 has an engine size of 1395cc. The car tax for this size of engine is £100.

Remember to think about the kind of values you will be **L** entering in the spreadsheet. Apply validation rules to each column range so that inappropriate data cannot be entered. (See pages 89 and 90 for validation rules.) For example, for the cars we are considering in this activity, the tax may vary between £100 and £150.

MOT

If the used car is more than three years old then it must pass the annual MOT (Ministry of Transport) test each year. The cost of an MOT test is £37.60. This figure has been included in the spreadsheet for Car 2.

Insurance

There are many factors that determine how much you will be charged for your car insurance. For our portfolio activity, these factors fall into two groups; those that are constant and those that vary depending on the individual car. The constant factors include: whether it is kept in a garage, driveway or on a public road, your postcode, your age, your driving experience, your occupation, the use for the car, the estimated annual mileage and the type of cover required – fully comprehensive or third party, fire and theft. The variable factors include the exact make and model of the car. Quotations can be obtained directly over the Internet or by researching through insurance dealers.

In your report, record which Internet search engines you used to locate car insurance companies. Record also the search strings you used in the search engines.

Compare the results of the quotations obtained from the Internet with the actual payment information obtained from current car owners in the questionnaire.

Depreciation

The graph on page 22 show clearly that as a car gets older, its value falls. This is called the depreciation. Normally, the depreciation cost is not the same each year; the value of a new car falls quite rapidly but, as the car becomes older, the fall in price each year is less. When calculating the cost of running a car for a year, we should also take into account this fall in value.

Example: If Car 2 was the used VW Polo example as on page 21, then, for £5000 we would be able to purchase a 1996 model. The average price for a 1996 model was £4909 and the average price for a 1995 model was £3707. During the year this represents a fall of £1202 (£4909-£3707).

When inserting depreciation data into our 'running costs' spreadsheet we are exchanging data between spreadsheets. This procedure should be automated so that changes to the source data are reflected by changes in our running costs sheet.

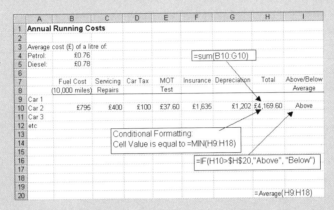

In column H, the total running costs for each car is calculated with the 'average' cost recorded below the list (in this example in row 20).

Column I uses an IF function (see pages 78 to 80) to show whether the running cost is above or below the average figure.

There is conditional formatting set on the cells containing the running cost totals in column H (see pages 72 to 74 for conditional formatting). The formatting is set to shade the cell with the lowest running cost figure, using the MIN function. Note, this needs to be an automated procedure as changes in the fuel costs (cells B4 and B5) will alter the running costs for the individual cars.

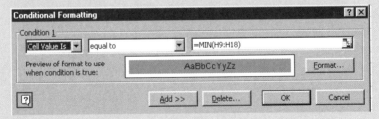

Using the results in the spreadsheet, a chart can be made to illustrate the relative running costs for each of the cars. This can be further refined to show the 'costs per week' by dividing by 52 or the 'costs per mile' by dividing by 10 000. The chart below shows the running costs of ten cars. The depreciation cost has been removed so that the figures show the actual money required to keep the car on the road.

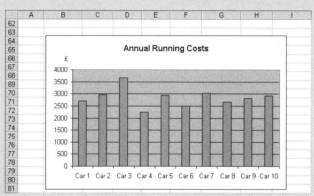

Presenting the activity

The spreadsheet tables and the charts should be printed together with your written explanation of the activity. The results from your spreadsheets and the associated materials on each of the cars should enable you to evaluate your work and make clear recommendations.

When word processing your report, make use of styles to give consistent formatting to the body text and headings. Using the header styles will also allow you to build a contents section automatically (select the Insert menu, and choose Index and Tables). Add illustrations to your report by scanning pictures from car brochures and importing from the Internet and clip art libraries. Also, add a header and footer to include, for example, the project title, your name and page number.

You must ensure that you proofread your work carefully and make full use of the spellcheck facilities. Supporting material may be placed in appendices of the report, but do ensure that it is relevant and keep such material to a minimum. As your project develops, ask your friends and your teacher at regular intervals to look at the work and suggest alternative ways of presenting the information and even suggestions of other aspects to include.

The content of your activity should be both interesting and relevant to other sixth form students, so a copy of the project could be passed to the school or college library. Selected parts of the report could be made available on the school intranet or on the network shared documents area for other students to access.

The visual data associated with this project makes it ideal for a multimedia presentation to your class. For example, Microsoft® PowerPoint slides can be prepared to take the audience through the stages from selecting the cars to calculating the running costs. The final recommendations can then be based on the costs, together with other relevant information researched during the project. When preparing the presentation slides, only include the key bullet points with the minimum of text. A printout of the presentation slides can be submitted as an appendix in your main report.

For students who are considering buying a car, either in the near future or the longer-term, it is likely that some financial help may be needed from their parents/guardians. This activity will have highlighted the very significant costs, not only of buying a car, but also of the running costs involved. It will show parents that you have researched the subject thoroughly and are aware of the full financial implications.

In this substantial activity, the full requirements for the portfolio would be met. Information has been collected and processed for several purposes. These were to obtain a list of desirable used cars, using a questionnaire, to determine the cost of each model according to the year of manufacture and establish the annual running costs for each car. The two audiences included fellow students, using the multimedia presentation to discuss the advantages and disadvantages of different makes of car, and the full report for parents to show that you have a sound understanding of the running costs involved.

Sample assignment checklist

Candidate's name: CANDY DATE

Title: Given £5000, what car could I buy and what would be the running costs?

Portfolio reference/page number: REF	Centre: 12345

Assignment 1: Assignment

Every box in one column must have an entry tick (or page reference) to show it has been done.

	Assignment 1	Teacher's initials
IT3.1 Plan and select information		
A Plan and use different sources to search for, and select, information required for **two** different purposes	✓	GW
A₁ My first purpose: To obtain a list of desirable cars which can be purchased with the money available	✓	GW
A₂ My second purpose: To calculate the running costs of the cars	✓	GW
B Plan how to obtain and use the information required to meet the purpose of your activity	✓	GW
C Choose appropriate sources and techniques for finding information and carry out effective searches	✓	GW
D Make selections based on judgements of relevance and quality	✓	GW
IT3.2 Develop information		
E Explore, develop and exchange information, and derive new information, to meet **two** different purposes	✓	GW
E₁ My first purpose: To determine the purchase costs of different used cars	✓	GW
E₂ My second purpose: To determine the running costs of the different cars	✓	GW

		Assignment 1	Teacher's initials

F Enter and bring together information in a consistent form, using automated routines where appropriate ✓ *GW*

G Create and use appropriate structures and procedures to explore and develop information and derive new information ✓ *GW*

H Use effective methods of exchanging information to support your purpose ✓ *GW*

IT3.3 Present information

I Present information from different sources for **two** different purposes and audiences ✓ *GW*

I₁ My first purpose and audience: To produce a report and presentation for other students ✓ *GW*

I₂ My second purpose and audience: To produce a summary of my findings to my parents to show I understand the financial implications of owning a car ✓ *GW*

J Develop the structure and content of your presentation using the views of others, where appropriate, to guide refinements ✓ *GW*

K Present information effectively, using a format and style that suits your purpose and audience ✓ *GW*

L Ensure your work is accurate and makes sense ✓ *GW*

M Include at least one example using text ✓ *GW*

N Include at least one example using images ✓ *GW*

O Include at least one example using numbers ✓ *GW*

Confirmation that all aspects of Information Technology are complete:

Candidate's signature: Teacher's signature:

Candy Date *Gareth Williams*

Date: 7/3/02 Print name: GARETH WILLIAMS

Part 3

Level 3 IT skills

Word processing

This section looks at some of the features of the word processor that enable more advanced tasks to be carried out by students. For example, the mailmerge facility (a useful technique to include in the Key Skills portfolio) is detailed. Performing a mailmerge task is also sometimes one of the questions in the Key Skill Level 3 examination.

In the Microsoft® Office suite of programs, many of the features are available across two or more packages. For example, many of the graphics features are common to Microsoft® Word, Excel and Publisher. Because of these common features, the skills learnt in one package can easily be applied in another program.

Remember, leaving aside for a moment the many special features involved with the presentation of the work, the word processor is used for writing text. This writing should be as free from errors as possible and it is important to proofread your work carefully. Some people find that the best way of proofreading text is to read the text out loud, taking care to read each word. Of course, this may not always be possible, especially in school or college! You should always use the spellcheck facility of the software and also, where possible, ask others – your friends, teachers or family – to read through your work. These tasks of proofreading, using the spellchecker and getting others to check your work are emphasised in the Key Skills course and are important procedures to learn for the future.

The topics included in this section on word processing are:

- Bullets and numbering
- Fields
- Graphics
- Mailmerge
- Styles
- Templates.

Bullets and numbering

Generally, **bullet points** are used when text is made up of a list of words, sentences or short paragraphs and you wish to show these as a series of points or statements. Bullet points, rather than numbering, can be used when the statements are in no particular order of importance.

Highlight the text and then click on the bullet point icon on the tool bar:

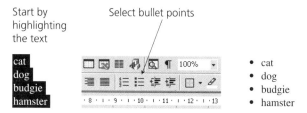

If you prefer a different style of bullet then highlight the text to which you wish to apply bullet points. Select Format from the menu bar, then select Bullets and Numbering. Choose a different type of bullet from the seven displayed or choose one to customise. If you choose to customise, you will be presented with a large number of symbols to use from a selection of font styles.

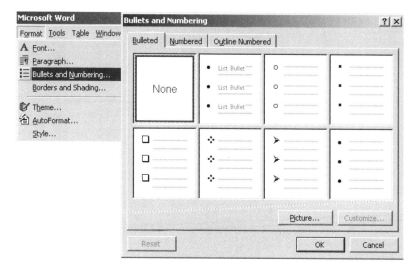

Some popular choices of bullet point are illustrated below:

- ❑ useful with checklists
- ✓ to show items completed
- ☞ decorative
- 🖳 decorative (IT).

Numbering is used when the text should be followed through in a particular order. For example, a list of instructions, or to label sections of a list of points so that you can refer to a particular part by its number.

Highlight the text to be numbered. Select the number icon from the tool bar.

A new number is generated for each new line of text after the enter key has been pressed. If a number has been given to a line of text where it is not required, highlight the individual line and, with the mouse, click the number icon again to switch it off.

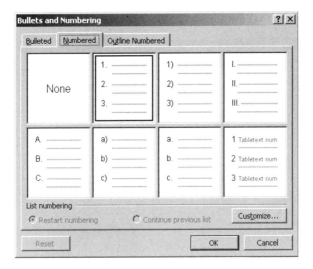

Fields

The word processor stores information about each document. This information includes:

- Date and time:
  - when created
  - when printed
  - when saved
  - today's date.
- Document information:
  - author
  - file size
  - number of words
  - number of revisions made
  - file name
  - number of characters
  - page number
  - total number of pages.

These, and many more pieces of information, can be automatically displayed in your document by inserting a field. All the different fields can be obtained from the Insert menu by selecting Field. The most useful fields to insert into a document are page numbers, date and file name. (Sometimes candidates are requested to insert these fields in the Key Skills IT examination.) The method for inserting the information into the header or footer is slightly different and is shown below.

Inserting page numbers, date and file name into the footer

If you are going to display the file name of your document in the footer, ensure your document has a name. If it is a new document, save the document first to ensure that it has a file name.

In the following example, the file name is presented on the left of the footer, the page number in the centre and the date on the right-hand side. The user can select the position and content of the fields.

Select View from the menu bar and then choose
Header and Footer.

Select the icon to move to the footer.

Switch between header and footer

When the footer is displayed, the cursor is flashing on the left. To insert the file
name at this position, select Insert AutoText and choose Filename.

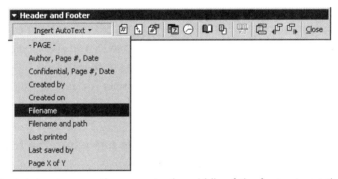

Press the tab key to move the cursor to the middle of the footer. Insert the page
number by selecting Insert AutoText and choosing Page.

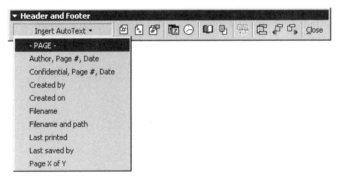

Press the tab key to move the cursor to the right of the footer. To insert the
date, click on the Date icon, as shown on the next page.

Insert date

The advantage of using fields rather than typing the information in directly is that they will update automatically. Page numbers will increment as the document grows, the file name will change if the file is saved under a different name and the date will always display the current date.

Graphics

There are two types of graphics that can be used to enhance documents:

- **drawings** which are part of the word processor
- **pictures** that are created outside the program.

The first part of this section deals with drawing objects in Microsoft® Word.

Drawings

Drawings are created with the Microsoft® Draw tool bar. The quickest way to obtain this tool bar onscreen is to select the icon on the standard tool bar, as shown on the right.

Drawing tool bar icon

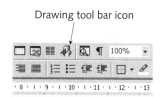

The facilities available from Microsoft® Draw include a range of AutoShapes, curves, lines and WordArt drawing objects. The tool bar also provides the means to colour objects and give them patterns and borders. The illustration below shows the tool bar and some of the AutoShapes available.

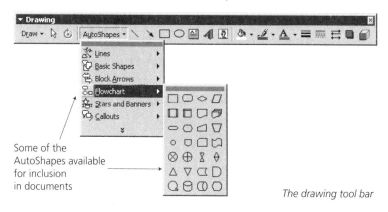

Some of the AutoShapes available for inclusion in documents

The drawing tool bar

To create an object, select the shape with the mouse and then draw it out to the desired size on the screen by holding down the left button of the mouse. As well as moving shapes around the screen, they can be resized, rotated, flipped, coloured and combined with other shapes. When creating a flowchart, where several shapes are joined by lines, the grid facility makes it easier to construct the picture more accurately. These features are available through the Draw icon.

When you select the 'Grid' option ensure that the 'Display gridlines on screen' check box is ticked

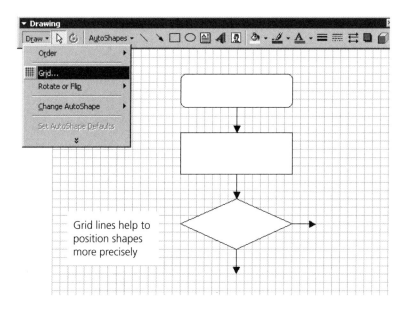

Another useful feature is to group together the separate shapes so that they can be manipulated as one picture. To do this, choose the 'pointer' icon and pull open a box by holding down the left button of the mouse. Ensure that all the objects that need to be grouped are selected. Then select the Group command from the Draw icon menu. This is illustrated in the diagram on the following page.

Select the 'pointer' icon and draw a box around the separate shapes,
eg start at the top left corner and move the mouse to the bottom
right corner while holding down the left button of the mouse

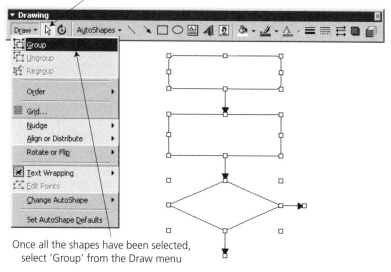

Once all the shapes have been selected,
select 'Group' from the Draw menu

When drawing objects are
created and moved over the text
in a document, the default
'wrapping style' is 'in front of
text'. This means that the text
will be hidden by the shape.
Wrapping is the name given for
how the text forms around the
graphic. In the Draw menu of
the Microsoft® Draw tool bar,
choose Text Wrapping and
change to square and notice the
effect. Experiment with the
other options. (Note, ensure the
drawing object is selected first.)

Text wrapping controls how the text will
form around the graphic image

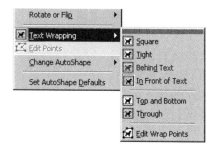

Pictures

Pictures from a variety of sources can be inserted into a word processed document. They may be bitmap images from the Microsoft® Paint program, scanned images, photographs from digital cameras or clip art images. Most imported images cannot be ungrouped but the clip art pictures are made from metafiles that can be ungrouped. When images are ungrouped, they can be converted to drawing objects and manipulated and enhanced with the facilities provided on the Microsoft® Draw tool bar. Microsoft® Word also comes with its own extensive library of clip art.

Inserting a picture

Select Insert from the standard tool bar and choose Picture. In this menu you are offered the choice of inserting From File or Clip Art. When the picture loads into Word, the picture tool bar should also be displayed. (Hint: If you need a tool bar that is not in view, click on View and select Toolbars, or right click with the mouse on any existing tool bar.)

The picture tool bar has commands that enable the picture to be cropped, to add borders, to adjust the brightness and to vary the contrast. The default text wrapping when pictures are inserted is 'inline'. In order to perform some of the actions on the picture tool bar, for example, adding a border, the text wrapping must be changed to another style.

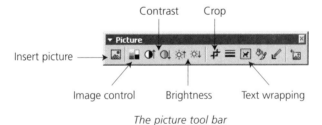

The picture tool bar

All graphics, whether drawings or pictures, can be stacked on top of each other. The order in which the graphics appear can be controlled from the Microsoft® Draw tool bar. Each object can be selected and moved up or down a level or sent to the top or bottom of the stack.

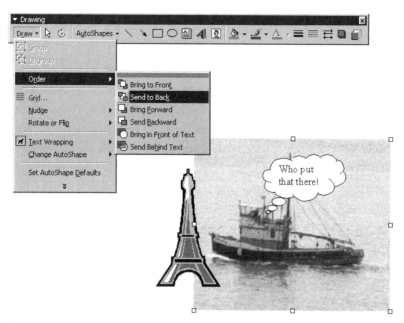

Mailmerge

Mailmerge is used to create letters, labels or print envelopes. In order to mailmerge a letter, two parts are required before the merge can take place. The first is a standard (or form) letter where the personalised parts of the letter, for example, the name and address of the person receiving the letter, are inserted with field names. The second part is a table of data to supply the data for the field names. The diagram below illustrates this process:

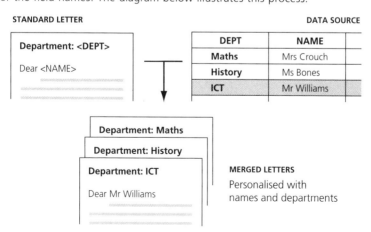

STANDARD LETTER

Department: <DEPT>

Dear <NAME>

DATA SOURCE

DEPT	NAME	
Maths	Mrs Crouch	
History	Ms Bones	
ICT	Mr Williams	

Department: Maths

Department: History

Department: ICT

Dear Mr Williams

MERGED LETTERS
Personalised with
names and departments

Starting a mailmerge letter

To carry out a mailmerge, click on Tools and select Mail Merge. The Mail Merge Helper box will now guide you through the three steps of the mailmerge procedure.

Start by clicking on the Create button for the main document. Choose the Form Letters option. You are now given the choice of creating the letter in the active window or in a new main document. Choose the Active Window button.

Creating the mailmerge data

Now move down to the second stage, the data source. Click on the button Get Data. From the four options presented, choose Create Data Source. The data that will be used by the mailmerge letters will now be created in a separate document in the form of a table. The Create Data Source box, as in the illustration below, is used to create the field names for the first row of the table.

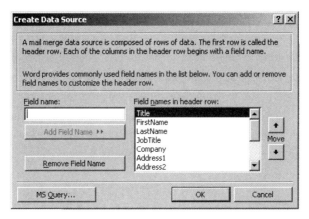

A list of field names is given. To remove field names from the list, select them and then click on the Remove Field Name button. To add new field names, type them into the box and click on the Add Field Name button. For example, you may wish to add a field for initials instead of first name or delete the field State and add County instead. The order of the fields can be changed by selecting one of the fields in the list and using the up and down buttons on the right of the box. Click on the OK button to finish. You will then be asked to provide a file name for saving the data.

You will notice that the Mail Merge tool bar now appears on the Word screen.

Note on addresses

In the majority of mailmerge applications, an address is entered so that it can be printed on the letter, mailing labels or envelopes. Addresses vary in size considerably, but it is generally sufficient to hold the address in four fields with a fifth for the postcode. The field names used to hold addresses are often:

- Address 1 (house name/house number and street name)
- Address 2 (house number and street name, if not in the Address 1 field, district, or can be left blank)
- Town/City
- County
- Postcode (referred to as 'PostalCode' in the program).

A choice is now offered to edit either the data source (add data to be merged) or the main document (start the mailmerge letter). To add data, choose Data Source.

The Data Form entry box now allows you to input data that will be saved in the mailmerge data file. The illustration below shows a sample of data entered for field names that provide the basic name and address fields. (The tab key should be used to move from one field to the next in the record.)

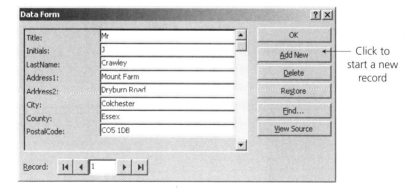

Click to start a new record

To return to this data entry form at any time, select the Edit Data Source icon at the right-hand end of the mailmerge tool bar and then select the Edit button under the data source section.

The data is stored in a Word table in the data document. Each row of the table contains one record with the top row holding the field names. Selecting View Source on the data form window will show this table:

Title	Initials	LastName	Address1	Address2	City	County	PostalCode
Mr	J	Crawley	Mount	Dryburn	Colchester	Essex	CO5 1DB

Designing the letter

Having created the data, we now need to create the mailmerge letter. Select the Mail Merge Helper icon from the mailmerge tool bar and click on the main document Edit button.

Now write the letter, but instead of typing in the person's name and address, insert the field names. Separate field names on the same line by using the space bar.

Merging the letter and data

Once the letter has been completed, the mailmerge can take place. This is done using the commands on the mailmerge tool bar. The merged document can be sent directly to the printer or it can be made to form a new document.

Mail Merge

Of course, a mailmerge with only one or two data records will not save a great deal of time. However, for a business, the mailmerge operation could generate hundreds or thousands of personalised letters automatically.

Styles

In the same way that we might say that a person has a particular style of writing, we can apply different styles to text in a word processor. Using a style is a quick way of applying a whole set of separate steps to the text. For example, changing the font type, size and alignment in one action.

Styles are particularly useful in longer documents like coursework projects. Using styles ensures that the titles, subtitles and body text look consistent throughout the document, but they also allow features such as the contents pages to be generated automatically. Another useful feature is the ability to modify a style and then apply this to the document. Any text linked to the style will automatically change its appearance to match the changes made.

When we start using the word processor, the normal template (see pages 49 and 50) defines the default style. The normal style is generally set to a font such as Times New Roman or Arial, with a font size of 11 or 12 points.

To change the style, highlight the text and select a new style from the style list, for example, a Heading 1 style, as illustrated on page 48.

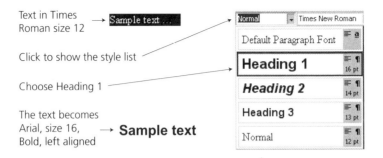

Text in Times Roman size 12 → Sample text...

Click to show the style list

Choose Heading 1

The text becomes Arial, size 16, Bold, left aligned → **Sample text**

The word processor in Microsoft® Office 2000 has over 100 styles defined in the normal template. The majority of these do not appear in the style list but can be seen by selecting Format from the standard tool bar and then selecting Style. The style box shows the full list of different styles and allows the user to modify existing styles or create new styles of their own.

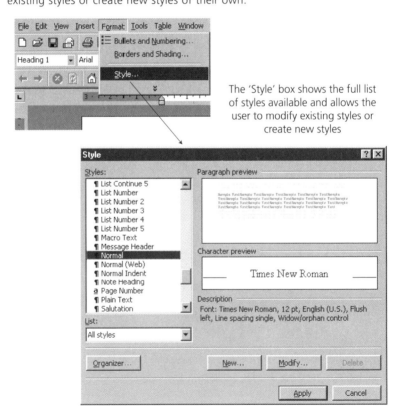

The 'Style' box shows the full list of styles available and allows the user to modify existing styles or create new styles

A style consists of two main parts – the character and the paragraph.
The character defines the font style, size and whether it is bold or italic.
The paragraph defines how the text is aligned (ie left, centred, right or justified), the tab stops, the line spacing and borders.

Templates

All documents are based on a template. The template determines the structure for the document and includes the:

- fonts available
- menu choices
- different tool bars available

- icons on the tool bars
- page layout
- macros (see pages 65 to 67).

When the word processor is started, a default template is loaded called the normal template. The Microsoft® Office package also provides a number of other templates to suit specific kinds of documents. These documents might include business letters, faxes or memos. The templates provided with the word processor are stored in a templates folder on either the hard drive of the workstation or on the network fileserver.

To load a new template, click on the File menu and select New.

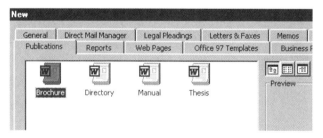

A variety of templates are supplied with Microsoft® Office

It is also possible to design your own template. This may be used to create a standard structure for a document. For example, a letter heading with your own address and perhaps a graphic image. Then, whenever a letter is needed, the new template is loaded. It is also possible to customise the menus and tool bars of the word processor.

Creating a new template as a letter heading

To create a new template as a letter heading, open the word processor and click on File, then select New. Select the Template option button in the bottom right corner of the New box.

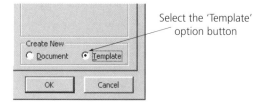

Select the 'Template' option button

You will now see that the name in the top left corner says 'Template1'.

Now prepare the letterhead and save the template. When you wish to use the letterhead, choose File, select New and then choose the new template and open it, this time as a new document.

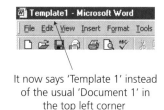

It now says 'Template 1' instead of the usual 'Document 1' in the top left corner

The Windmill
Flacks Green
Terling
Essex
CM3 2QW

Databases

This section covers the following topics:

- Designing a database
- Queries
- Reports

- Macros
- Validation.

A database is a program that stores data. It can then be used to search and sort the data and to print out reports. In this section we will look at how to perform these techniques by using queries, reports and macros in Microsoft® Access.

To illustrate some of these features, a sample database has been designed. This database is used by a yacht magazine to hold details of the boats they offer for sale. The data held in the database is structured in the form of a table. The columns of the table represent the database fields and the rows represent the records of the database. In Microsoft® Access, it is possible to have two or more tables that are linked. However, this sample database only uses one table of data.

(A copy of the data used in this database is provided on the Pearson Publishing Web site at http://www.pearsonpublishing.co.uk/publications/extras/.)

Designing a database

The fields required in our sample database are code, model of boat, category, length of boat, year of build, type of engine, price and telephone number. These fields are displayed below together with the type, size and description:

Field name	Field type	Field size	Description
Code	Text	3	Unique code number (primary key)
Model	Text	30	Model of boat
Category	Text	10	Category of boat (power, sail, etc)
Length	Number (Integer)		Length of the boat in feet
Year	Number (Integer)		Year when the boat was made
Engine	Text	20	Make and size of engine
Price	Currency		Price in sterling
Telephone	Text	15	Seller's telephone number

Each boat in the database has its own unique code and this field is made the primary key field using the key symbol.

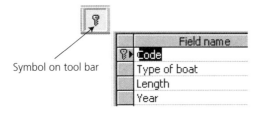

Symbol on tool bar

Note: When designing a database it is important to make a list of the information that you will need to obtain from it. For example, in the boat database on page 51 there would be no way of searching for wooden boats as there is no field which specifies the material from which the boat is made. In the examples used later in this section, the database will be used to:

- search for a boat's details by its reference code
- search for boats less than a particular price
- search for a boat by year and price
- search for boats with two types of engine
- print out a price list sorted by category then price.

Queries

Queries are used to extract data from the database tables. When designing a query, the user can choose which fields to show, set conditions on which records are selected and also sort the records.

The data that is obtained when a query is run is based on two factors, the fields that are selected and the search criteria that filters out some of the records. The illustration on page 53 shows how these two factors reduce the data returned from the query. If no search criteria are applied then data from all of the records is returned when the query is run.

Fields selected to be displayed by the query

Code	Model	Category	Length	Year	Engine
liv	Classic Estuary Cruiser	Power	23	1960	Lister 18hp
nsu ←	Jaguar 24	Sail	24	1990	Honda 10hp
nus ←	Leisure 23	Sail	23	1979	
nuw	Rinker 25	Power	25	1989	Mercury 260hp
oaq	Fletcher Arrowflyte GTO	Power	14	1993	Mercury 60hp
obt	Vimar 504	Power	17	1994	Mariner 60hp
ofr	Fletcher Zingaro	Power	28	1987	Ford 130hp
ogu	Falcon 22 SPC	Power	24	1987	BMW 220hp
ohr ←	Wing 25	Sail	25	1965	Albin 12hp
ohv	Wilson Flyer 17	Power	17	1997	Yamaha 75hp
oit ←	Hunter Sonata 23	Sail	23	1986	Mariner 5hp

Criteria imposed
by the Query:
Category = 'Sail'

The data that is shaded
is returned when the
query is run

Results from running
the query

Jaguar 24	24	1990
Leisure 23	23	1979
Wing 25	25	1965
Hunter Sonata 23	23	1986

*Effect of the query – Select the fields Model, Length and Year from the boats
database table where the Category = 'Sail'*

Query: Enter the search condition when the query is run

Sometimes it is useful to apply the query criteria at the point when the query is
run rather than build it into the query design. For example, in the boats database,
entering the reference code when prompted as the query is run can access a
single record. In the example below, we will show all the fields for the reference
code selected.

Select Queries, and double-click on
Create query in Design view. In the
Show Table box, click on the Add
button, then close the Show
Table box.

In the top panel of the Query window, click with the mouse on the * at the top of the list of fields in the table. Holding the left mouse button down, drag the * down into the field row in the first column. Now select the Code field and drag that down into the field row of the second column and untick the Show box. Select the criteria row of the second column and enter open and close square brackets [ ].

Selecting the * and dragging into the 'Field' row gives all the fields in the table

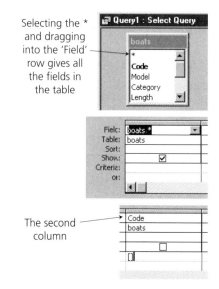

The second column

Note:

1   An alternative to dragging down fields is to double-click on the field in the table.

2   The double square brackets will prompt the user to enter the data when the query is run. You can enter instructions inside the brackets to assist the user, eg [Please enter the boat code].

Now run the query by selecting the exclamation sign [!] . The square brackets in the criteria row under the reference ensure that the user is prompted for the parameter value.

User is prompted for a parameter value:

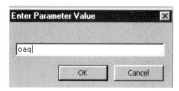

Results of the query

	Code	Model	Category	Length	Year	Engine	
▶	oaq	Fletcher Arrowflyte GTO	Power	14	1993	Mercury 60hp	

Finish by saving the query.

Query: Single condition and sort

In this example, we will see how we can use a query to extract data from the table using a single condition in the criteria row and present this data in order. From the boats database, this query will provide the code, name and price for all boats under £5000. The boats will be sorted in order of price.

Start a new query and add the table to the top panel of the query window. Instead of bringing down all the fields, drag down Code into the field row of the first column, Model into the second column and Price into the third column.

Field:	Code	Model	Price	
Table:	boats	boats	boats	
Sort:				
Show:	☑	☑	☑	

Note: An alternative to dragging the fields down, or double-clicking, is to click into the field row cell and select the field from the displayed list.

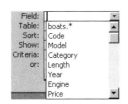

In the column for Price, select:

• the criteria cell and enter **<5000**

• the sort cell and select **Descending**.

Field:	Code	Model	Price
Table:	boats	boats	boats
Sort:			Descending
Show:	☑	☑	☑
Criteria:			<5000

When the query is run [!], the boats under £5000 will be displayed in descending order of price.

Code	Model	Price
ohv	Wilson Flyer 17	£4750.00
obt	Vimar 504	£4600.00
oss	Drascombe Lugger	£4500.00
ovq	Orkney Coastline 14	£3000.00
oaq	Fletcher Arrowflyte GTO	£2200.00
ouo	Ballerina	£1950.00

Query: Multiple conditions (AND)

In this example, we will see how we can use a query to extract data from the table using a multiple AND condition in the criteria row. From the boats database, this query will provide the code, name, year and price for all boats between £10 000 and £15 000, not older than 1990.

Start a new query and add the table to the top panel of the query window. Enter the following fields: Code into the field row of the first column, Model into the second column, Year in the third column and Price in the fourth column.

In the column for Year, select:

- the criteria cell and enter **>=1990**.
  (greater than or equal to the year 1990)

In the column for Price, select:

- the criteria cell and enter **>=10000 AND <=15000**.
  (greater than or equal to £10 000 and less than or equal to £15 000)

Field:	Code	Model	Year	Price
Table:	boats	boats	boats	boats
Sort:				
Show:	☑	☑	☑	☑
Criteria:			>=1990	>=10000 AND <=15000

Note: To obtain an AND relationship, both conditions should be on the same line

When the query is run ▮ , the boats between £10 000 and £15 000 built in 1990 or later are displayed.

Code	Model	Year	Price
oyw	Parker 24	1992	£14,995.00
nsu	Jaguar 24	1990	£12,500.00

Query: Multiple conditions (OR)

In this example, we will see how we can use a query to extract data from the table using a multiple OR condition in the criteria row. From the boats database, this query will provide the code, name and engine for all boats with a Volvo or Honda engine.

Start a new query and add the table to the top panel of the query window. Enter the following fields: Code into the field row of the first column, Model into the second column and Engine into the third column.

In the column for Engine, select:

- the criteria cell and enter **Like "*Honda*" OR Like "*Volvo*"**
  (The * is a wild character that means any text or numbers. The quotation marks will be inserted by the program if you forget to insert them.)
  You can add a space after 'like' and after 'OR'.

Because the Engine field contains other data, eg the size of the engine, it is necessary to include the * wild characters which, in this case, will accept any characters in front of, or after, the word.

Field:	Code	Model	Engine
Table:	boats	boats	boats
Sort:			
Show:	☑	☑	☑
Criteria:			Like "*Honda*" OR Like "*Volvo*"
or:			

When the query is run ❗ , the boats with Honda or Volvo engines will be displayed.

Code	Model	Engine
pzo	Hardy Family Pilot 20	Honda 45hp
okp	Birchwood 25	Volvo 115hp
pwt	Fairline 21 Weekend	Volvo 200hp
oqp	Swift 18	Honda 4hp
oyp	Fairline Weekender	Volvo 130hp
oxx	Dragon DK408	Honda 10hp
nsu	Jaguar 24	Honda 10hp

If an OR condition is required between two different fields then the second condition is written on the 'or' row, beneath the criteria row.

Query: Criteria with dates
Matching a particular date

To find a particular date from a field in a database, insert the date in the criteria row enclosed by # signs.

Field:	Date
Table:	Table1
Sort:	
Show:	☑
Criteria:	#13/07/01#
or:	

Matching part of a date

To find all the records in a database where the date in the date field matches a particular month. For example, this could be used to search the date of birth field of club members to see who has a birthday during a particular month.

A single 'm' means take the month part of the date as a number, ie 1 to 12

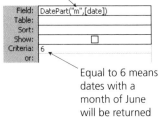

Equal to 6 means dates with a month of June will be returned

The function DatePart can be also be used for locating particular days and years as well, ie:

- to locate a particular day, the expression becomes: **DatePart("d",[date])**

- to locate a particular year, the expression becomes: **DatePart("yyyy",[date])**.

Note that when a function like 'DatePart' is used, it should be entered into the field row.

Selecting between two dates

To find all the records in a database between two dates, we can use the Between expression. The dates can be entered directly into the query, as shown in the first illustration below, or the start and end dates can be entered when the query is run, as shown in the second illustration below.

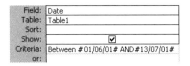

In this query, all the records between 1 June 2001 and 13 July 2001 are selected.

Here the user is prompted to enter a start date and then an end date when the query is run. Using this method gives greater flexibility and the query can be used to generate data for a report. The text inside the square brackets can be any explanation which will help the user to input the correct data.

Adding and subtracting with dates

It can be useful to add or subtract with dates, for example, the field holding a person's date of birth could be subtracted from the current date to show their age. The illustration below shows how a library could use a database query to show who has overdue books.

The current date (today's date) is given in the database by the function date(). In the example shown, an overdue book is when the book has been on loan for more than seven days. We can write this as:

Today's date-Date when the book was lent out >(greater than) 7

In the database, this would become:

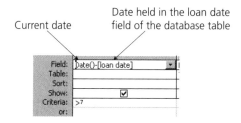

Current date

Date held in the loan date field of the database table

Other query criteria
Yes/No field criteria

In the queries above, we have looked at criteria that select data from text fields, number fields and date fields. Another common field used in the design of databases is the 'Yes/No' field, also known as a Boolean field. For example, this field might be used to record whether a club member has paid their membership:

Field Name	Data Type
Membership Paid	Yes/No

A 'Yes/No' field can only have one of two values and is called a Boolean field

The query criteria to search for all members that have not paid their membership is shown on the right:

Field:	Membership Paid
Table:	Table1
Sort:	
Show:	☑
Criteria:	False
or:	

'False' will select the members that have not paid. 'True' will select those who have paid

Criteria based on the contents of fields in a form

Later in this section we will look at how to produce reports from the database and how to place command buttons onto forms. One very useful feature when designing a database is to be able to print a report for the record showing on the screen. For example, a button on the form of the boats database could be selected to print out all the details of the boat being viewed. The information that is printed by the database report can be based on the data extracted by a query. The query shown below will only select the record that is currently being viewed by the form. (The name of the form is 'frmboats' in this example.)

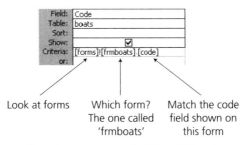

Look at forms   Which form?   Match the code
The one called   field shown on
'frmboats'   this form

Note the separator symbol '!' and '.' used
between the square brackets

Reports

The reports function is used for displaying data from the database on the computer screen or sending it to the printer. The first step in creating a report is to decide what data is required to be presented. The report can be based on a database table, in which case, all the data in the table can be shown in the report. More usually, the report is based on a database query that has already extracted specific data from the database. The first example report is taken from the boats database (see page 51).

Produce a price list of boats

The price list will include all the boats in the database and so the report will be based on the table. The fields displayed in the price list will include the boat code, model, category, year and price. The list will be sorted by price within their category of groups (ie sail and power).

Select Reports and choose the Create report by using wizard icon. In the Report Wizard box, ensure that the report is based on the boats table. Select each field that is required in the report and move it across to the right-hand box using the single chevron button, then select the Next button.

Highlight the field in the left-hand box and move it across to the right

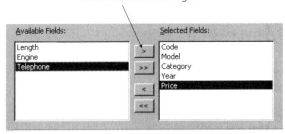

The next Report Wizard screen asks 'Do you want to add any grouping levels?'. For our price list, we wish to group the boats by category, ie Sail and Power. Select category and move to the right.

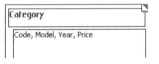

The next Report Wizard screen asks 'What sort order and summary information do you want for detail records?'. We wish to list the boats in order of price, from the highest to the lowest in each category. In the first box, using the arrow to show the fields, choose the Price field. Click on the order button so that it shows Z to A. Select the Next button.

Select 'Price' from the list of fields

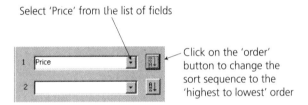

Click on the 'order' button to change the sort sequence to the 'highest to lowest' order

The next Report Wizard screen asks 'How would you like to lay out your report?'. Under Layout, choose the option button Align Left 1 and under Orientation, choose Portrait. (When more fields are selected to show in the report it may be necessary to select Landscape.)

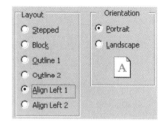

The Report Wizard screen then asks 'What style would you like?'. This is really up to the user, but in the illustration of the finished price list shown below the 'Corporate' style was chosen. Give your report a name and select the Finish button.

Boats

Category		Power			
	Price	*Code*	*Model*		*Year*
	£14,995.00	oyw	Parker 24		1992
	£14,600.00	nuw	Rinker 25		1989
	£14,000.00	ogu	Falcon 22 SPC		1987
	£12,950.00	pys	Tamar 2000		1985
	£12,500.00	oyp	Fairline Weekender		1987

Creating a report from a query

In this report we shall print out a list of all the sailing boats between 20 ft and 25 ft in length. (Traditionally, boats tend to be measured in feet, hence we have followed this convention.) The report will show details of the model, length, year, engine, price and the seller's telephone number. The list will be ordered by length and the report will show the average price for the group of boats.

Start by designing the query (see pages 52 to 60). The design should be similar to the illustration below:

In the first screen of the Report Wizard, select the new query to base the report on. Move all the fields across to the right-hand box.

Base the report on the new query

Tables/Queries

Query: qrysail20to25

Available Fields:

Model
Length
Year
Engine
Price
Telephone
Category

As the fields needed were selected in the query, use the double chevron to move all the fields to the right-hand box

At the Grouping Levels screen, choose to group by category. At the Sort screen, choose to sort by length. Select the summary options and tick the average box for price, as in the illustration below:

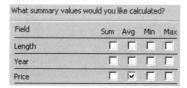

What summary values would you like calculated?

Field	Sum	Avg	Min	Max
Length	☐	☐	☐	☐
Year	☐	☐	☐	☐
Price	☐	☑	☐	☐

At the layout screen, choose Align Left 1 and Landscape.

Choose a style (in the illustration of the report below, the 'Corporate' style has been used) and a suitable name for the report before finishing.

Boats 20-25

Category	*Sail*					

Length	*Model*	*Year*	*Engine*	*Price*	*Telephone*
22	Ballerina	1991	Mariner 6hp	£1,950.00	01856 775569
23	Hunter Sonata 23	1986	Mariner 5hp	£6,750.00	01720 712296
23	Leisure 23	1979		£6,500.00	01288 770715
23	Seamaster Sailor 23	1984		£6,900.00	01236 732993
24	Jaguar 24	1990	Honda 10hp	£12,500.00	01485 272749
24	Vivacity	1977		£5,750.00	01663 831881
25	Wing 25	1965	Albin 12hp	£6,500.00	01362 210011

Summary for "Category" = Sail (7 detail records)

Average   *£6,692.86*

Modifying a report design

By selecting the design tool 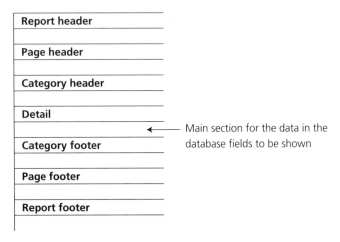, it is possible to modify the design of the report. The report is structured into a number of bands, for example:

Report header
Page header
Category header
Detail
Category footer
Page footer
Report footer

Main section for the data in the database fields to be shown

Within the bands there are label boxes and text boxes. The label boxes are used to hold the report titles. The text boxes are generally bound to the database fields. These boxes can be moved around the report or deleted. New boxes can also be added.

A common request in the Key Skills examination at Level 3 is to insert the student's name, date and a report title in the footer of the report. This can be done in either the Page Footer section or the Report Footer section. To add this detail:

- Drag down the Report Footer bar, making more room in the Page Footer section.

- From the tool box, select the Label Box icon and drag open a box in the Page Footer section.

Select the label box to insert your name and report title

Often, the date is included in the footer of a report generated by the Report Wizard. If it has not been, select the Insert menu and select the Date and Time option.

Inserts current data

Boxes which print in the footer of each page in the report

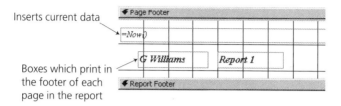

Macros

A macro is a set of one or more commands that can be made to automate the different procedures in the database. For example, a simple macro could be used to open a form or to print out a report. Macros may be activated from buttons placed on a form, which makes the database operations very easy to use.

Using a macro to print a price list

In this example, we shall produce a macro to print out a price list (model, code, age and price fields) of just the sailing boats in our database. This procedure consists of several steps:

1 **Designing the query** – The criteria required in the query is 'category = sail'. This is illustrated below:

Field:	Category	Model	Code	Year	Price
Table:	boats	boats	boats	boats	boats
Sort:					
Show:	☐	☑	☑	☑	☑
Criteria:	="sail"				

2 **Designing the report** – The report is based on the query shown above (qrySail). At the sort screen of the Report Wizard, choose price in descending order and choose a suitable title for the report (Sail Price List).

Report based on the query

Just the fields required for the price list

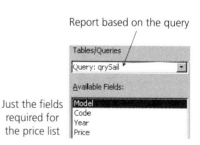

Tables/Queries

Query: qrySail

Available Fields:
Model
Code
Year
Price

Sail Price List

Price	Model	Code	Year
£17,500	MacGregor 26	oqs	1998
£13,750	Westerley Centaur	plo	1985
£12,500	Jaguar 24	nsu	1990
£9,500	Elizabethan 29	pnt	1979
£6,900	Seamaster Sailor 23	ons	1984
£6,750	Hunter Sonata 23	oit	1979
£6,500	Leisure 23	nus	1979
£6,500	Wing25	ohr	1965
£5,750	Vivacity 24	phq	1977
£5,500	Swift 18	oqp	1991
£4,500	Drascombe Lugger	oss	1981

3 **Creating the macro** – To create the macro to select and print the price list, start by selecting the Macros button and choose New.

In the top left Actions box, select Open Report. In the lower area, specify the name of the report to open and to send to the printer.

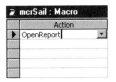

Lower area…

Select the name of the report

| Report Name | Sail Price List |
| View | Print |

Choose here whether to print or view onscreen

Creating a button for the macro

Buttons are usually placed on forms. In this example, the button will be created on the basic form created by the Report Wizard for entering data but, as the facilities of the database grow, a separate form can be created with buttons for different processes. (Macros can be created to move between forms.)

In Form Design View, select the button from the tool box, and, using the mouse, drag out a button onto the form.

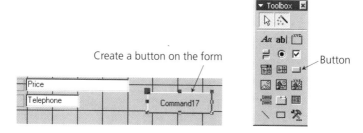

Create a button on the form

Button

As the button is created, the screen changes to the Command Button Wizard. From the categories box, select the Miscellaneous category and then choose Run Macro from the Actions box, followed by Next. In the next screen, choose the name of the macro to run – in our case, the macro 'mcrSail'.

The next screen of the Command Button Wizard asks 'Do you want text or a picture on the button?'. Choose the text option button and type in 'Sail Price List'.

Choose Next to move to the last screen where you are asked to give a name to the command button, eg 'cmdSail'. Select the Finish button.

A command button has now been created that will run the macro to print out the sail boat price list. To test this button, the form must be in Form View, not Design View.

Validation

Checking or validating the data that a user types into a database is important. The person who creates the database (in this case, you), should also create some validation rules as they design the fields and tables.

In the table design, under the General tab, there are two entries relating to validation. The first is the validation rule and the second is the message that will appear on the screen to help the user if the data entered breaks the rule.

Consider the fields of the boats database:

Field name	Field type	Field size	Description
Code	Text	3	Unique code number (primary key)
Model	Text	30	Model of boat
Category	Text	10	Category of boat (power, sail, etc)
Length	Number (Integer)		Length of the boat in feet
Year	Number (Integer)		Year when the boat was made
Engine	Text	20	Make and size of engine
Price	Currency		Price in sterling
Telephone	Text	15	Seller's telephone number

Text fields

The first validation rule we can apply would be to the category field. All boats would fall into a limited number of categories, for example, power, sail or dinghy.

To apply a validation rule that would only allow these entries, we would enter the Design View of the table, select the 'Category' field. In the Validation Rule box, type ="Power" Or ="Sail" Or ="Dinghy".

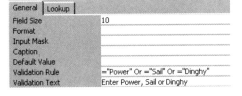

Notes:

1   The text has also been added in the Validation Text to help the user if they enter an incorrect entry to this field.

2   When using validation rules, text is enclosed by quotation marks (").

Number fields

Another validation rule we could apply to the boats database is on the 'Year' field. Here we might wish to stop years being entered that are before (less than) 1950 or after

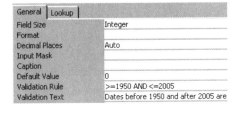

(greater than) 2005. To do this, select the 'Year' field in the Design View of the table and insert the rule **>=1950 AND <=2005**.

If a date outside this range is now entered, the following error message appears:

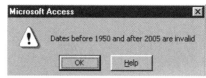

Note: When using validation rules, numbers should not be enclosed by quotation marks.

Other forms of validation

Input masks can be used to control the way data is entered. These are special characters that are entered

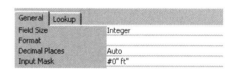

for a field in the box marked Input Mask under the General tab. A detailed description of all the input mask patterns is beyond the scope of this handbook, but an example for the boats database is illustrated above.

This input mask allows one or two digits to be entered, ie lengths up to 99 feet. The " ft" means that the abbreviation 'ft' for feet will be displayed automatically after the number.

Prevent duplicate entries can be used on some fields, for example, where a unique number is allocated to a field. These fields are often used as the primary key. To apply this rule to a field, select the field in Design View of the table, and under the General tab set the Indexed box to Yes (No Duplicates):

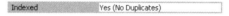

Require that data must be entered may be necessary for some fields, for example, in the boats database you may not wish the model of boat field to be left empty. To apply this rule to a field, select the field in Design View of the table, under the General tab set the Required box to Yes:

Spreadsheets

This section covers the following topics:

- Cell references: Absolute and relative
- Conditional formatting
- Charts
- Headers and footers
- IF function
- Lookup function: Vertical and horizontal
- Macros
- Naming sheets and cells
- Printing options
- Validation.

Cell references: Absolute and relative

A reference identifies a cell or range of cells in a worksheet and enables the data contained in the cell to be used in formulae. The top left cell of a spreadsheet is in column A and on row 1, so its cell reference is A1. If you wanted to reference a range of cells then you would give the cell reference for the top left cell and for the bottom right cell of the group and insert a colon in-between, as shown below:

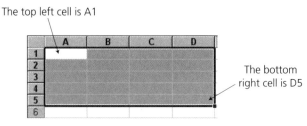

The top left cell is A1

The bottom right cell is D5

The reference for the group of 20 cells shown is A1:D5

Depending on the task that you wish to perform in the spreadsheet, the references can be either **relative** or **absolute**. To make an absolute cell reference, a dollar sign ($) is placed in front of the letter or the number, or both. The main difference between absolute and relative references is when a cell is copied. The illustration below shows this:

	A	B	C	D	E
1	6				
2					
3					
4		=A1			
5					
6					
7					
8					
9					

In cell B4, the relative reference to cell A1 is entered. When the enter key is pressed, cell B4 will display the number 6.

Cell B4 is then copied horizontally to E4 and vertically to B7. The copied cells no longer display the number 6 that is in cell A1. This is because the reference has automatically adjusted as the cell is copied.

Cell values

	A	B	C	D	E	F
1	6					
2						
3						
4		6	0	0	0	
5		0				
6		0				
7		0				
8						
9						

Cell formulae

	A	B	C	D	E
1	6				
2					
3					
4		=A1	=B1	=C1	=D1
5		=A2			
6		=A3			
7		=A4			
8					
9					

When the dollar sign is placed in front of the column letter, this ensures that the referenced column does not change when the cell is copied. When the dollar sign is placed in front of the row number, this ensures that the referenced row does not change when the cell is copied. The illustration on page 72 shows a dollar sign placed in front of both the column letter and the row number, but in some tasks only one dollar sign may be needed.

In cell B4, the cell reference to cell A1 is now made an absolute reference by inserting dollar signs in front of both the column letter and row number.

	A	B	C	D	E
1	6				
2					
3					
4		=$A$1			
5					
6					
7					
8					
9					

Now when cell B4 is copied horizontally and vertically, the cell reference continues to refer to cell A1 and each of the copied cells displays the number 6.

Cell values

	A	B	C	D	E	F
1	6					
2						
3						
4		6	6	6	6	
5		6				
6		6				
7		6				
8						
9						

Cell formulae

	A	B	C	D	E
1	6				
2					
3					
4		=$A$1	=$A$1	=$A$1	=$A$1
5		=$A$1			
6		=$A$1			
7		=$A$1			
8					
9					

Relative references adjust automatically as you copy them. Absolute references always refer to a specific location on the sheet and copying does not change this. Cells and ranges of cells can be given name references (see pages 85 to 87). These are always absolute references.

Conditional formatting

A cell in a spreadsheet can be formatted to make it stand out in the sheet. Formatting includes the font style, size and colour, underlining, borders, shading and patterns. When conditional formatting is used, the format of cells can be made to change automatically depending on the contents of the cell. In the spreadsheet shown on page 73, an example is given of a hospital waiting list:

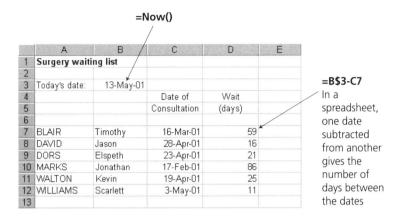

=Now()

	A	B	C	D	E
1	Surgery waiting list				
2					
3	Today's date:	13-May-01			
4			Date of	Wait	
5			Consultation	(days)	
6					
7	BLAIR	Timothy	16-Mar-01	59	
8	DAVID	Jason	28-Apr-01	16	
9	DORS	Elspeth	23-Apr-01	21	
10	MARKS	Jonathan	17-Feb-01	86	
11	WALTON	Kevin	19-Apr-01	25	
12	WILLIAMS	Scarlett	3-May-01	11	
13					

=B$3-C7
In a spreadsheet, one date subtracted from another gives the number of days between the dates

Cell B3 contains the current date, generated by the spreadsheet function (=Now()). Column D shows the number of days the person has been waiting for surgery since their consultation with a doctor. It is important that people do not wait too long for surgery, so, in this example, we shall use conditional formatting to shade the cell if the number of days exceeds 60.

To apply conditional formatting, highlight the required cells, choose Format and select Conditional Formatting.

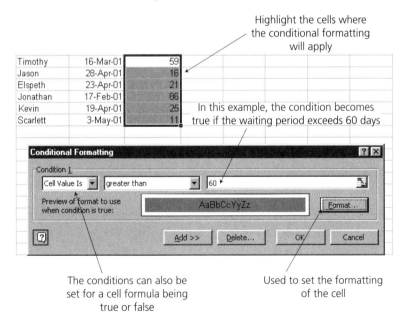

Highlight the cells where the conditional formatting will apply

In this example, the condition becomes true if the waiting period exceeds 60 days

The conditions can also be set for a cell formula being true or false

Used to set the formatting of the cell

The result of applying conditional formatting is that Jonathan Marks' waiting period is now shaded and stands out clearly in the sheet. If more than one condition needs to be applied, click on the Add button in the Conditional Formatting box and put in the second condition.

	A	B	C	D	E
1	**Surgery waiting list**				
2					
3	Today's date:	13-May-01			
4			Date of	Wait	
5			Consultation	(days)	
6					
7	BLAIR	Timothy	16-Mar-01	59	
8	DAVID	Jason	28-Apr-01	16	
9	DORS	Elspeth	23-Apr-01	21	
10	MARKS	Jonathan	17-Feb-01	86	
11	WALTON	Kevin	19-Apr-01	25	
12	WILLIAMS	Scarlett	3-May-01	11	
13					
14					

The 'Wait' exceeds 60 days

To see which cells have had conditional formatting applied to them, go to Edit and select Go To. Click on the Special button and select the option button called Conditional formats.

Charts

When groups of numbers are displayed visually as a graph or chart, it is often much easier to see a trend in the figures. A spreadsheet such as Microsoft® Excel makes this very easy to do using the Chart Wizard.

Types of chart

Seven of the 12 different chart types from a Microsoft® Excel spreadsheet are shown below:

Column charts illustrate how data changes over a period of time or shows the comparison between different items. Column charts can be shown in 3D (three-dimensions). Data can be stacked in the column to show how the parts make up the whole.

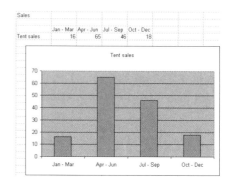

74

A **bar chart** illustrates comparisons between different items. The bars lie horizontally to emphasise the comparisons and not changes over time like the column charts.

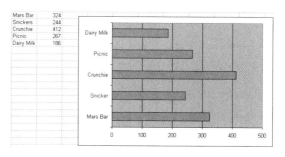

Note: Bar charts illustrated in Maths textbooks are column charts in the spreadsheet.

Line charts (graphs) show the trends in data. The data is shown at equal intervals along the horizontal axis.

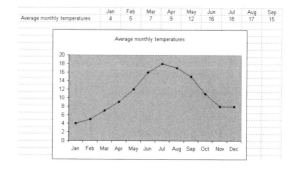

Area charts emphasise the size of the change in data with time. The total is shown together with all the contributing parts.

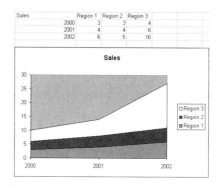

In **pie charts**, for each of the data items shown in the chart, the size of the slice in the pie chart represents the proportion that item is of the whole. Slices can be pulled out of the 'pie' to emphasise their importance. In the

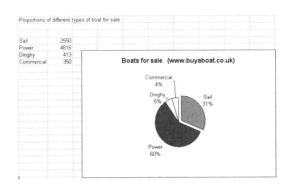

illustration, the slice representing sailing boats has been pulled out.

Stock charts are useful for showing share prices. The price of shares rises when they are in demand and falls if the company is not doing so well. This chart shows the current share price set against the maximum and minimum levels the price has reached over a period of time. These charts can also be

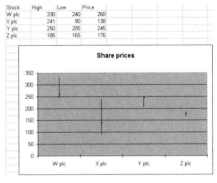

used for scientific data, such as variations in temperature.

The **XY (scatter) chart** shows the relationships between sets of data values. (The chart in the illustration below shows how a fence 60 m long set out in a rectangular shape has the maximum area when the length of a side is 15 m.) XY (scatter) charts are used for scientific and mathematical data.

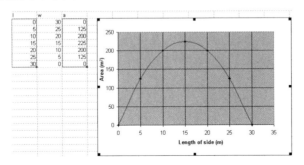

Chart detail

The Chart Wizard takes the user through a series of steps, from choosing the type of chart to its final appearance. The graph below shows some of the options available to the user, including adding titles, grid lines and legends or keys.

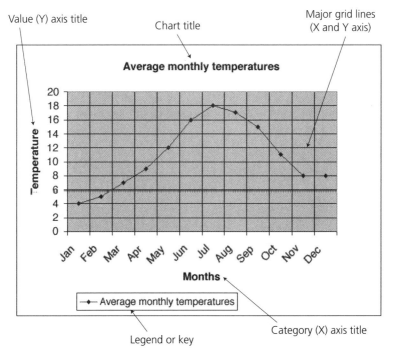

It is also possible to select finer (minor) grid lines, change the position of the caption, add data values to the points on the chart and alter the patterns, colours and borders of the chart.

Making a chart

Highlight the data in the spreadsheet that is required for the chart. This should include the text headings, as these will become the axis labels. Select the Chart Wizard:

If the data items to be plotted on the chart are in columns (or rows) with other data between then highlight the first column, hold down the CTRL key before highlighting the second column. Holding the CTRL key down stops the first column from losing highlighted status.

Headers and footers

Before printing your spreadsheet, you should always add your name to the work, particularly in a classroom of networked computers where several similar sheets may be sent to the printer at the same time. The sheet footer is an ideal place to include your name, together with other useful information, such as the date, file name and page number.

Click on File, select Page Setup and then choose the Header/Footer tab.

Choosing either the Custom Header or the Custom Footer buttons divides the section into a left, centre and right area and provides icons for inserting the page number, date, time and file name. The illustration below shows an example of a footer containing the information usually requested in the Key Skills examination, ie a name, date and title.

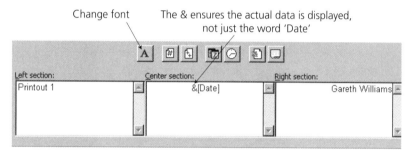

Creating a footer

IF function

The IF function will return one value if a condition is true and another value if the condition is false. The function has three parts, each separated by commas, for example:

IF(condition, value_if_true, value_if_false)

An example of this function is shown below. It has been used to determine whether a student has passed or failed a test with a pass mark of 60%.

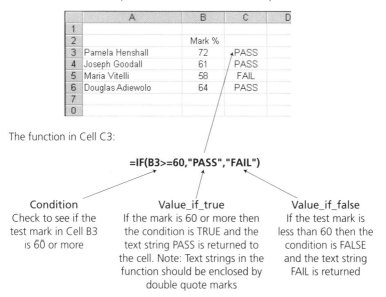

The function in Cell C3:

=IF(B3>=60,"PASS","FAIL")

Condition	Value_if_true	Value_if_false
Check to see if the test mark in Cell B3 is 60 or more	If the mark is 60 or more then the condition is TRUE and the text string PASS is returned to the cell. Note: Text strings in the function should be enclosed by double quote marks	If the test mark is less than 60 then the condition is FALSE and the text string FAIL is returned

The 'Value_if_true' and 'Value_if_false' can be text strings, formulae or functions. The following example illustrates a more complex IF function to calculate a salesperson's rewards for high sales.

Example

A salesperson needs to sell over £10 000 of goods per month to receive a £250 bonus. If they sell over £15 000 of goods, they receive their bonus and 2% of the total sales:

A more complex IF function

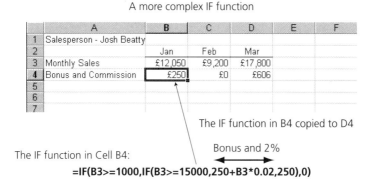

The IF function in B4 copied to D4

The IF function in Cell B4:

Bonus and 2%

=IF(B3>=1000,IF(B3>=15000,250+B3*0.02,250),0)

The inner IF statement is calculated if sales of more than £10 000 is TRUE. The second IF function checks to see if sales are more than £15 000. When one IF function is inside another, this is called 'nested'. Up to seven IF functions can be nested!

Lookup function: Vertical and horizontal

The lookup is a function that returns a value to the cell from a table of cells in another part of the worksheet. This is a useful function and can be used in a range of applications. For example, the marks of an examination are listed in column of a spreadsheet. For a GCSE examination these marks need to be converted into a grade, from A* to U. Typical grade boundaries might be:

- A*   87 – 100%
- A   77 – 86%
- B   67 – 76%
- C   56 – 66%, etc.

Using a lookup function, the spreadsheet will automatically insert the correct grade alongside each mark.

There are two types of lookup function: a vertical lookup (VLOOKUP) and a horizontal lookup (HLOOKUP). The more common one to use is the vertical lookup and that is the one to use for the examination marks example shown above.

Vertical lookup

The lookup function has four parts, each separated by a comma, ie:

VLOOKUP(value, table, table column, range)

The illustration on the next page shows how the function is used to provide the grades in the examination example.

The lookup function is entered into cell C4, then copied down to C18

Column 1 of the lookup table shows the highest mark required to achieve the grade, eg a mark of 40% is not high enough to achieve a D grade but is in the range for the E grade

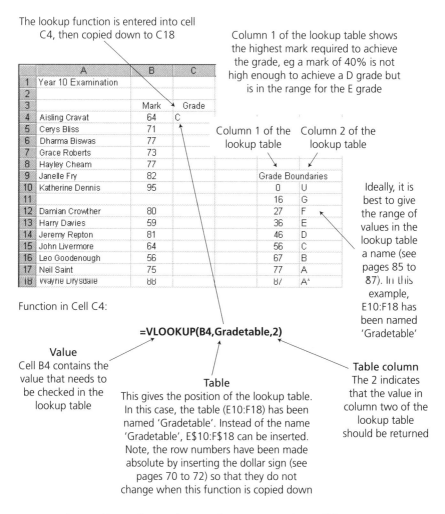

Column 1 of the lookup table

Column 2 of the lookup table

Ideally, it is best to give the range of values in the lookup table a name (see pages 85 to 87). In this example, E10:F18 has been named 'Gradetable'

Function in Cell C4:

=VLOOKUP(B4,Gradetable,2)

Value
Cell B4 contains the value that needs to be checked in the lookup table

Table
This gives the position of the lookup table. In this case, the table (E10:F18) has been named 'Gradetable'. Instead of the name 'Gradetable', E$10:F$18 can be inserted. Note, the row numbers have been made absolute by inserting the dollar sign (see pages 70 to 72) so that they do not change when this function is copied down

Table column
The 2 indicates that the value in column two of the lookup table should be returned

- **Value** – This can be a value, a reference to another cell (as in the example of the examination marks and grades) or a text string.

- **Table** – This is the table of information where the data is looked up. The value that is being checked is always compared with the data in column 1 of the lookup table. If the range value has been left off or is set to true (see page 82) then the data in this first column must be sorted into ascending order.

- **Table column** – This number determines from which column of the lookup table the data will be taken and returned to.

- **Range** – This is a logical value, ie true or false, and it is optional. If it is true, or omitted, then an exact match between the data in column 1 of the lookup table and the value is not required. This is the case with the examination data: many of the marks fall between the values shown in column 1. When this happens, the row selected is the one with less than the value. If the range is set to false, then an exact match between the value and the data in column 1 of the lookup table is required. An example of using a lookup function with exact matching is a lookup table of food items and prices. When the name of the item is entered into a cell, the price is returned from the lookup table.

Horizontal lookup

The horizontal lookup works in the same way as the vertical lookup, but the value in the table will scan across the first row instead of down column 1 of the lookup table. The example below for discount air fares shows a horizontal lookup table in use.

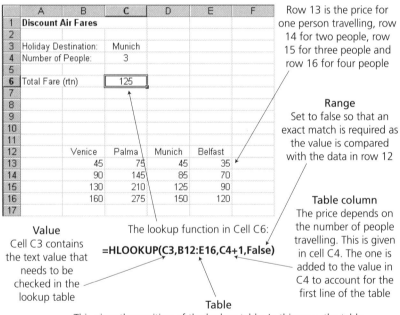

Row 13 is the price for one person travelling, row 14 for two people, row 15 for three people and row 16 for four people

Range
Set to false so that an exact match is required as the value is compared with the data in row 12

	A	B	C	D	E	F
1	Discount Air Fares					
2						
3	Holiday Destination:		Munich			
4	Number of People:		3			
5						
6	Total Fare (rtn)		125			
7						
8						
9						
10						
11						
12		Venice	Palma	Munich	Belfast	
13		45	75	45	35	
14		90	145	85	70	
15		130	210	125	90	
16		160	275	150	120	
17						

Value
Cell C3 contains the text value that needs to be checked in the lookup table

The lookup function in Cell C6:

=HLOOKUP(C3,B12:E16,C4+1,False)

Table column
The price depends on the number of people travelling. This is given in cell C4. The one is added to the value in C4 to account for the first line of the table

Table
This gives the position of the lookup table. In this case, the table (B12:E16) has been entered directly rather than given a name. Making the cell reference absolute is not necessary in this example as the lookup function is not being copied to other cells

82

When the fourth part of the lookup function is set to false for an exact match to be found, the data in the first column (for vertical lookups) and the first row (for horizontal lookups) does not need to be placed in order.

Macros

A macro is used to automate a series of commands and functions. A macro can be made by setting the macro to record and then proceeding manually through the series of steps. The recording is then switched off and the macro stored. When the same process needs to be repeated, the macro, which has captured the process, is run.

Once a macro has been made, it can be run by a combination of keystrokes or by placing a button on the screen and making the macro activate when the button is pressed.

Macros can be used to automate quite simple processes like moving to another part of the sheet or sending data to the printer. They can also be used to apply complex functions and formulae to data. The example below shows how a macro is made to change to a new sheet and a button can be inserted on the sheet to run the macro.

Example

A teacher uses a spreadsheet to keep the class lists and marks for their classes. Each year group is recorded on a different sheet in the workbook.

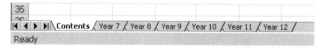

When the spreadsheet is loaded, the first worksheet to show is called 'Contents'. We shall build a macro to move to another worksheet. The contents of the sheet we wish to move to must be named so that it can be referred to during the recording of the macro. To give the area of a sheet a name, highlight the cells and type the name into the Name Box in the top left corner of the screen.

Recording a macro

Click on Tools on the tool bar and select Macro. Choose Record New Macro and enter a name for the new macro. In this example, the macro is called 'mcrYr12'.

Give the macro a name

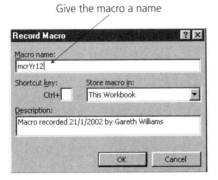

All the operations carried out are now recorded and stored in the macro until the Stop Recording button is pressed.

The Stop Recording button

In our example, the macro is going to record the action of moving to the 'Year 12' worksheet. To do this, select the down arrow on the Name Box and choose 'Year12'.

Name box

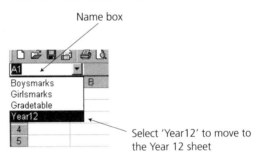

Select 'Year12' to move to the Year 12 sheet

In our very simple example, the macro is only recording this one action. In a complex procedure, macros will record many operations.

Now the Stop Recording button is pressed. (If this is not visible onscreen, it can be found under the Tools menu. Select Macro and Stop Recording.)

Adding a button to activate the macro

On the first sheet, called 'Contents', we can place a button that will run the macro and move directly to the correct sheet for Year 12. (In a full version of the spreadsheet there would be a button for each year.)

Right click with the mouse on a tool bar on the screen to obtain the full list of tool bars. Select the Forms tool bar. Click on the Button icon and, on the sheet, drag open a button while holding down the left button of the mouse.

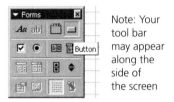

Note: Your tool bar may appear along the side of the screen

As the mouse button is released, the Assign Macro box will appear on the screen. Select the macro to work with the button, in this example, the mcrYr12 macro, and press OK.

Change the label on the button

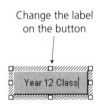

Year 12 Class

The default label on the button will be 'Button 1'. This can be changed to a more useful name, in this case – 'Year 12 Class'.

Now click off the button and then select it with the mouse to check that the macro works. (It may be useful to add another button on the 'Year 12 Class' worksheet to move back to the 'Contents' sheet.) To change any of the properties of the button, for example its label, right click on it.

Naming sheets and cells

When the spreadsheet, Microsoft® Excel, is started, a workbook is opened. Each workbook generally starts with three worksheets, with 'Sheet 1' open on the screen. Sheets can be added, deleted or renamed.

To change the name of a sheet, right click on the sheet tab and select Rename. Type in a new name for the sheet.

To add, delete or rename a sheet,
right click on the sheet tab

Worksheets have been
renamed in this illustration
of a teacher's markbook

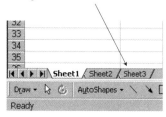

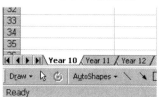

A cell in a spreadsheet can be referred to by its column and row heading. For example, A1 ('A' for column, '1' for row) refers to the top left cell of the sheet. Individual cells and groups of cells can be given names to make the sheet more understandable. The illustration below shows some examination marks for a Year 10 class.

To find the average mark for the girls in cell B20, we could enter the formula:

=AVERAGE(B4:B10)

However, if we named the range of cells, B4 to B10, as 'Girlsmarks' the formula would become:

=AVERAGE(Girlsmarks)

	A	B	C
1	Year 10 Examination		
2			
3		Mark	
4	Aisling Cravat	64	
5	Cerys Bliss	71	
6	Dharma Biswas	77	
7	Grace Roberts	73	
8	Hayley Cheam	77	
9	Janelle Fry	82	
10	Katherine Dennis	95	
11			
12	Damian Crowther	80	
13	Harry Davies	59	
14	Jeremy Repton	81	
15	John Livermore	64	
16	Leo Goodenough	56	
17	Neil Saint	75	
18	Wayne Drysdale	88	
19			
20	Girls Average Mark		
21	Boys Average Mark		
22	Class Average		

This makes the formula more understandable. It can be particularly important in a large and complex sheet with many calculations.

To name a cell or group of cells, highlight the cells, then go to the left-hand box on the tool bar and type in a name.

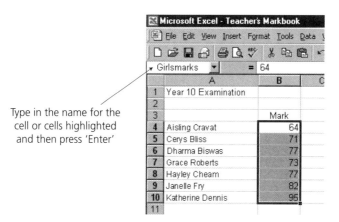

Type in the name for the cell or cells highlighted and then press 'Enter'

Printing options

When we come to print a spreadsheet, there are a number of options available that may be relevant to the work. The most common of these are:

- changing the paper from portrait to landscape
- selecting an area of the sheet to print
- printing the row and column headings
- repeating rows and columns on each page
- printing the gridlines
- scaling (shrinking or expanding) the sheet to fit the paper.

Changing the paper to landscape

Click on File and select Page Setup. Choose the Page tab and select the Option button for landscape.

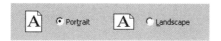

Selecting portrait or landscape

Selecting an area of the sheet to print

If a spreadsheet document is sent to the printer, the sheet will print from cell A1 in the top left corner of the sheet. Sometimes the sheet, or portion of the sheet, you wish to print is situated in columns to the right or in rows further down the sheet.

To print a specific part of a spreadsheet, highlight the section and click on File and select Print Area. Then choose Set Print Area.

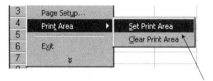

To set an area for printing

Printing the row and column headings

When you need to refer to specific cells of a spreadsheet, it can be useful to print out the column headers (A, B, C, etc) and the row numbers (1, 2, 3, etc) from the left-hand side. Click on File and select Page Setup. Choose the Sheet tab and tick the Row and Column Headings check box.

Repeating rows and columns on each page

When a large spreadsheet is printed, the content of the cells may be printed on two or more pages. It may not always be easy to identify what the data refers to if the title for the column was only printed on page 1. The option to repeat rows means that the column titles can be printed on each page and the option to repeat columns means that the row headers can also be repeated.

Click on File and select Page Setup. Under the Sheet tab, in the box labelled 'Rows to repeat at top:' enter the range of cells to repeat, as shown in the illustration below:

	A	B	C	D	E	F	G	H
1	Pupil	Last Name	First Name	Sex	Year of	Form	Year of	
2	ID				Entry		Departure	
3	5	ALTMAN	Marion	F	1995	B	2002	
4	6	APTED	Grace	F	1995	C	2002	
5	7	ASHTON	Emil	M	1995	S	2002	
6	8	BARKWORTH	Natalie	F	1995	A	2002	
7	9	BARTON	Emma	F	1995	D	2002	
8	10	BARTON	Gabriel	M	1995	D	2002	
9	11	BAZALGETTE	Rachel	F	1995	D	2002	
10	12	BEATON	Simone	F	1995	D	2002	
11	13	BENEDICT	Ralph	M	1995	B	2002	
12	14	BEWICK	Rodn	M	1995	C	2002	

Print titles

The column headings are in rows 1 and 2 so these are entered into the box (the dollar sign indicates that the rows are absolute)

Rows to repeat at top: $1:$2

Columns to repeat at left:

In the example on page 88, the names continued onto several pages so it was useful to have the headings printed on each page. The lower box for 'Columns to repeat at left:' can be used for wide sheets.

Printing the gridlines

A very useful feature when printing is to output the gridlines of the spreadsheet. This ensures that data can be read accurately, even across wide rows in landscape mode. It is also useful to print the gridlines when selecting to print the row and column headers.

Click on File and select Page Setup. Choose the sheet tab and tick the Gridlines check box.

Scaling the sheet to fit the paper

Sometimes a sheet may be slightly too large to fit on the page, even with the options of reducing the column widths, altering the font size or changing the orientation to landscape. The scaling option enables sheets to be enlarged or reduced in size. A normal print is 100%, and so 90% would represent a small reduction in both the width and height of the sheet.

Click on File and select Page Setup. Choose the Page tab and type in a scaling factor. Note, the option is also available to adjust the scaling automatically to fit one or more pages exactly.

Validation

It is important that the data that a user enters into a computer is accurate, otherwise the computer may produce some strange, and incorrect, results! Mistakes can occur for many reasons. For example, users may become tired or distracted in their work or they may find it difficult to read the handwritten copy of the data. When making a spreadsheet, the designer can apply validation rules to individual or groups of cells that will help prevent mistakes occurring when data is entered.

Applying validation

To apply validation, highlight the cell or group of cells. Click on the Data menu and select Validation. Under the Settings tab, choose the type of validation criteria for your cell(s). For example, if a particular group of cells were to hold the results of rolling two dice then the cells would be validated so that the user could only input a whole number between two and 12 (see the illustration below):

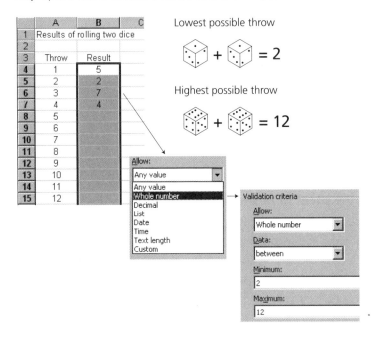

If a value is now entered into one of the cells that has been validated that is less than two or greater than 12, an error message will be displayed saying 'The value you entered is not valid'.

Validation can be used to ensure the user enters the correct data within the correct range. The data can be whole numbers (as in the example above), decimal numbers, dates, times or values from a list. The data validation window has two other tabs, these are:

- **Input message** – A message entered here will appear on the sheet when the cell is selected. This is useful for providing the user with instructions on the type of data to enter into the cell.

- **Error alert** – This allows the designer to customise the message displayed if a user enters data that is not allowed by the validation criteria.

Transferring data between programs

It is often necessary to transfer data between programs, for example, a chart produced in a spreadsheet may need to be passed to a word processor or the records of a database may be needed for a mailmerge operation. This section will look at the following transfers:

- Data text file (.txt) to word processor (Microsoft® Word)
- Data text file (.txt) to database table (Microsoft® Access)
- Data text file (.txt) to spreadsheet (Microsoft® Excel)
- Database query results to word processor table
- Database query results to word processor mailmerge
- Database query results to spreadsheet
- Database report to word processor
- Database report to spreadsheet
- Spreadsheet table to word processor
- Spreadsheet chart to word processor.

It is particularly important to learn how to import text data files as these are provided for you to work with in your examination. Often, there are several different ways of transferring data between packages. The methods illustrated in this section will demonstrate one way to achieve each of the data transfers listed above. Your teacher may show you alternatives; there are no right and wrong methods providing the end result is achieved.

Data text file to word processor

A text file holding data to be transferred into the word processor is unstructured in that commas do not separate the individual data items. Letters, memos and reports are examples of these files.

Open the word processor (Microsoft® Word). Choose File, Open. Having located the correct folder, ensure that the 'Files of type:' is set to display Text Files. Select the file and then Open.

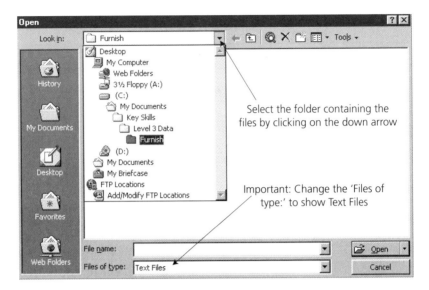

Select the folder containing the files by clicking on the down arrow

Important: Change the 'Files of type:' to show Text Files

When saving the new Word document, change the 'Save as type:' back to a Word document.

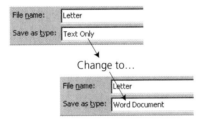

Change to...

Data text file to database table

A text file holding the data to be transferred into a database is structured so that the data for each field is separated, generally by commas.

Open Microsoft® Access as a blank database. You will be asked to enter a file name for the new database. In the examination, follow the instructions given in the question for this. Choose File, Get External Data, Import, as shown in the illustration on page 93.

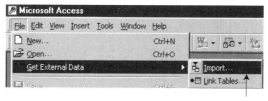

Use to import text data

This screen displays the folders and files and allows you to select the data file to import. Note: Change the 'Files of type:' to Text Files so that the text files will be displayed.

The Import Text Wizard now starts. The Wizard comprises six screens as follows:

1   If commas (or other similar characters) have been used to separate the data items, as in the Key Skills examination data, then accept the 'Delimited' button and move on to the next screen.

2   Here, the character that separates each data item can be chosen. In your examination data files this will be a comma, which is likely to be the default selection in the window. Before moving on to the next screen, tick the check box 'First Row Contains Field Names' if this is the case. With the files used for the examination, this box must be ticked.

Tick this box if the first line of the data file contains the headings. For the examination data the box must be ticked

3   Accept the option button selection 'In a New Table' unless you are adding new data to an existing table. (Note: In the examination, the scenario called 'HomeSrch' has two data files with similar structures, Prop1.txt and Prop2.txt (see page 100). If the question asked candidates to import both files into the same database table then the second option, 'In an Existing Table:' would be used for the second imported file.)

4 In this screen, you can specify information about each of the fields you are importing. You can move directly to the next screen, as changes can also be made in the Design View of the database table after the import process has been completed. Note: On this screen it is possible to select fields not to be imported by ticking the check box.

5 The next screen recommends you choose a primary key for the table. Sometimes the data itself will have a primary key field where the data in each record is unique, for example, a product number or customer number. In your examination, look carefully at the data file and read the question instructions carefully before making your choice here.

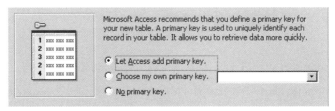

6 Choose a name for your table and select the Finish button. Again, in the examination you will be instructed on the name to use for the table.

Data text file to spreadsheet

A text file holding the data to be transferred into a spreadsheet is structured so that the data for each cell is separated, generally by commas.

Open the Microsoft® Excel spreadsheet. Choose File, Open and in the open window change the 'Files of type:' to Text Files.

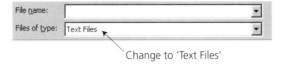

Change to 'Text Files'

Select the folder and text file required and click on the Open button. You will now be guided through the three steps of the Import Text Wizard:

1 Ensure that the option button 'Delimited' is selected if commas are used to separate the data (this will be the case in your examination files). This screen also enables data to be imported lower down the sheet if required.

2   Here the character that has been used to separate the data into different
    cells must be selected.

Select the 'Delimiter'

3   The final screen allows some limited formatting of the columns. As this can
    be after the data has been imported, there is no need to change settings at
    this stage. Click on Finish to complete the import.

Database query results to word processor table

In a Microsoft® Access database, run the query that selects the data to be
transferred. Highlight all the records in the query by holding down the ALT key
and pressing A, or by clicking with the mouse on the blank square in the top left
of the query table, as shown in the illustration below.

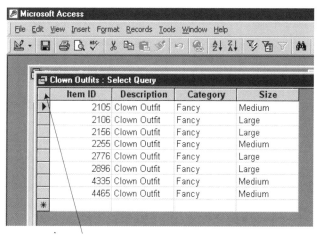

Select all the data by clicking in the corner square of
the query (or hold down the ALT key and press A)

Query selecting 'Clown Outfit' from the examination data – Clothes

Choose Edit and select Copy to pass the data to the clipboard. Change to the
word processor document and place the cursor where the results of the query
are required. Choose Edit and select Paste to insert the query table.

Database query results to word processor mailmerge

From Microsoft® Word, select Tools and then Mail Merge. The Mail Merge Helper window displays three parts for the merging process, creating the main document, choosing a data source and finally the merge. Before you can select the data source from the Microsoft® Access query, you must create the main document. Choose the Form Letters option and select Active Window.

Having created the document, click on the Get Data button and select Open Data Source.

The Open Data Source window will be displayed, change the 'Files of type:' to **MS Access Databases**, as in the illustration on the right.

Change to MS Access Databases

Select the folder and the Microsoft® Access database that contains the query you wish to use for the merge. Select the Queries tab in the Access window and choose the query. Having obtained the data source for the mailmerge, you will now be prompted to Edit Main Document.

Database query results to spreadsheet

In Microsoft® Access, select the Query. Choose Tools and select Office Links, then Analyze It with MS Excel, as in the illustration on the right.

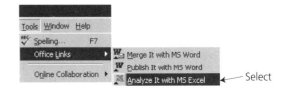

Select

This will create and open a spreadsheet displaying the contents of the query. The file name of the sheet will be the same as the query name.

If you want to transfer the results of a database query into an existing sheet, it is possible to copy and paste the data using the clipboard. If the data being transferred is longer than the cell width, the row height will increase. After widening the column(s) to accommodate the new data, the row heights should be adjusted using Format, Row and then AutoFit.

Database report to word processor

In Microsoft® Access, display the database report that is to be transferred to Microsoft® Word by double-clicking on it. From the tool bar, select the Office Links icon and choose Publish It with MS Word, as shown below.

Office Links icon — Select

This will create a Word document displaying the report. If the different parts of the report have been set out across the page, these will be replicated in Word using tab positions. Note that the new word processor document is in Rich Text Format, choose File, Save As and then change to Save as type: Word Document.

Database report to spreadsheet

In Microsoft® Access, display the database report to be transferred to Microsoft® Excel by double-clicking on it. From the tool bar, select the Office Links icon and choose Analyze It with MS Excel, as shown below.

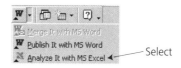

Select

This will create a Microsoft® Excel spreadsheet displaying the report.

Spreadsheet table to word processor

The transfer of data from the spreadsheet to a table in Microsoft® Word is easy to do by the copy and paste facility using the clipboard. In the Microsoft® Excel spreadsheet, highlight the cells containing the data to be moved into the word processor. Choose Edit and select Copy.

In the word processor, place the cursor at the point where the data is to be inserted. Choose Edit and select Paste. The data is inserted as a table in Microsoft® Word.

Spreadsheet chart to word processor

The chart in the Microsoft® Excel spreadsheet can be produced as an object on the sheet or as a new sheet that fills the spreadsheet screen. In either case, select the chart by clicking on it. In the case of the sheet chart, click near the edge of the screen to ensure you are selecting the whole chart.

Transferring the chart can be done through the clipboard, so choose Edit, then Copy in the spreadsheet. Open the Microsoft® Word document and choose Edit and Paste. The sheet may need resizing, which can be done by dragging in the corners. Remember, although the chart can be left, centre and right aligned, it may need the text wrap changing if you wish to move it around your document with the mouse (see page 41).

Part 4

The examination

The examination

For the examinations at Level 3 in Information Technology, you are required to use electronic data that is downloaded by the school. There are currently 12 sets of data and the examination is based around one of these sets. During the examination, which lasts one and a half hours, you will be asked to import the data into one or more software packages and perform a series of tasks. The examination paper is quite detailed and the instructions given need to be followed carefully.

The examination data is grouped in topic folders. Each folder contains text files containing the data to be used in the examination. All of the files are available to practise with before the examination, but you will not know which topic will be selected until you open your paper at the start of the examination. The 12 topic folders and files presented for use in the examinations from the start of 2002 are as follows:

Topic	Files (all .txt files unless indicated)
Art	Article, Pictures (also two graphic files Arts.jpg and News.jpg)
Cars	Data1, Data2
CDs	CDs, Stock
Clinic	Injuries, Patients, Talk
Clothes	Clothes, DayChrge, Income1
Driving	Dschool, Letter
Employ	Jobs, Stats
Euro-Sh	Data, Letter, Address
Furnish	Customer, Inventry
Holidays	Holidays, Rebates
HomeSrch	Letter, Prop1, Prop2
IT-Supp	Invoice, Software

The examination board may change these topics and data files in due course so it is important to check with your teacher which are the current data files. If you wish to download these files, they can be found at http://www.qca.org.uk/nq/ks/key-skills-data/.

At the start of the examination paper there is a short explanation of the scenario in which the data is used. This describes the meaning of codes used in the database fields. A similar description is included in the example examination paper shown in this handbook (see page 105).

The data files

The data files that will be needed in your examination may be of different types and structures, depending on the software package they are to be used with. Although you will have instructions on the paper as to which data file to use, it is useful preparation work to understand how the files can be imported and copied.

Database data

Database text files have data for each field which is separated by commas. The first line of data is the field (or column) headers. Text data is enclosed by quotation marks. An example of this data file is shown below.

The first line contains the field/column headers

All text data is enclosed by quotation marks

"Holiday No","Location","Activity","Departure Airport","No of Nights","Start Date","Departure Day".
"T101","Tenerife","Sailing","Manchester",7,21/6/02,"TH",300
"K101","Katmandu","River Rafting","Heathrow",21,18/11/02,"MO",1200
"T102","Tenerife","Volcano Exploration","Manchester",14,1/6/02,"TU",530

Each line of data represents a database record or row in the database table

Text file holding data – Most likely for a database program
(Taken from Holidays.txt)

Spreadsheet data

Spreadsheet text files are similar to the database text files. The data to go into the different cells of the spreadsheet are again separated by using commas. The file is likely to contain numeric data which can be manipulated in the sheet. Not all of the cells in a spreadsheet are filled, so a series of commas with no data between them is common. An example is illustrated on page 102.

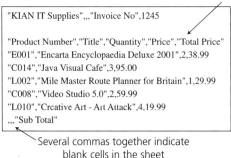

'Quantity' and 'Price' are given so the spreadsheet can be used to calculate the 'Total Price' (not given)

"KIAN IT Supplies",,,"Invoice No",1245

"Product Number","Title","Quantity","Price","Total Price"
"E001","Encarta Encyclopaedia Deluxe 2001",2,38.99
"C014","Java Visual Cafe",3,95.00
"L002","Mile Master Route Planner for Britain",1,29.99
"C008","Video Studio 5.0",2,59.99
"L010","Creative Art - Art Attack",4,19.99
,,,"Sub Total"

Several commas together indicate blank cells in the sheet

Text file holding data – Most likely for a spreadsheet program
(Taken from Invoice.txt)

Word processing/desktop publishing data

These text files contain unstructured text, not comma-separated data. They may be letters, memos or descriptions and are imported or copied into a word processor. An example of this type of text file is illustrated below.

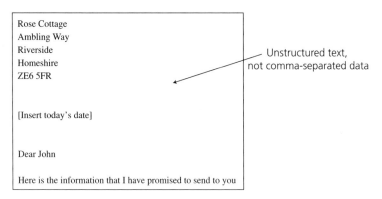

Rose Cottage
Ambling Way
Riverside
Homeshire
ZE6 5FR

[Insert today's date]

Dear John

Here is the information that I have promised to send to you

Unstructured text, not comma-separated data

Text file holding data – For importing or copying into a word processor

Images

An image file (.jpg) could be imported or copied into a word processor document, a spreadsheet or a database report.

Examination preparation checklist

The text files needed for the examination give clues to the questions that may be asked. The following is a checklist of skills to practise before you take the examination:

Database

- Import data from a text file into a database table. ☐

- Import more data with the same structure into an existing table. (For example, see data files Prop1 and Prop2 of HomeSrch.) ☐

- Design a query to extract information from a table (using single and multiply conditions). ☐

- Produce a report based on a query, grouping and sorting the data. ☐

- Change the footer in a database report to include new information, eg your name and a title. ☐

Spreadsheet

- Import data from a text file into the spreadsheet. ☐

- Import results from a database table or query. ☐

- Format cells, type, number of decimal places, borders, etc. ☐

- Create formulae in cells, eg: ☐

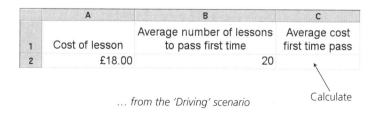

	A	B	C
1	Cost of lesson	Length of lesson (min)	Cost per hour
2	£18.00	45	

... *from the 'Driving' scenario*

Calculate

	A	B	C
1	Cost of lesson	Average number of lessons to pass first time	Average cost first time pass
2	£18.00	20	

... *from the 'Driving' scenario*

Calculate

	A	B	C
1	Job applicants	Jobs filled	Percentage jobs filled/ job applicants
2	3347	1769	

Calculate

... from the 'Employ' scenario

- Know how to apply 'discounts' or percentage changes to numbers. ☐
- Use the IF and AVERAGE functions. ☐
- Create a chart from the values in the sheet. ☐
- Transfer a spreadsheet table or chart to a word processor document. ☐

Word processor

- Format and align text. ☐
- Perform a mailmerge using database tables and queries for the data source. ☐
- Use the Insert Field facility to insert a date. ☐

General

- Produce a screen dump and paste into a word processor or desktop publishing program. ☐

Important note

The example examination paper that follows is based around one of the 12 sets of data that may be used in the actual examinations, but the way the data is used and the tasks performed with the data will be different in your examination.

Key Skills Information Technology Level 3

Example Question Paper

YOU NEED

- Access to a computer, software and a printer
- Access to the data files to support the scenario 'IT-Supp': Invoice and Software

You may use a bilingual dictionary

There are 3 tasks in this test

Task A (total 22 marks)

Task B (total 26 marks)

Task C (total 2 marks)

Try to complete ALL the tasks

YOU HAVE 1 HOUR 30 MINUTES TO FINISH THE TEST

Try to complete ALL the tasks

ENTER YOUR NAME ON EVERY DOCUMENT, PREFERABLY AS A FOOTER

Documents without a name will not be marked

KIAN IT Supplies

The theme for this example test involves working with a set of information relating to an IT Supplies company selling computer software. You will need to use software that has a database and a spreadsheet facility. You will be asked to

- import a given data file into a database table
- interrogate the database and produce a report
- import data representing an invoice into a spreadsheet
- print the final invoice after completing the formulae in the spreadsheet.

Information on about 55 software packages is contained in the data file **Software**. The invoice information to be imported into the spreadsheet is held in the data file **Invoice**.

Task A

1 In this task, you have to create a database using database software and a directory or folder structure in which to keep your files. The information for the database is provided in the data file **Software**.

    a   Create a new directory or folder called **IT Supplies**.

    b   The file name for the database must be the characters **D1-**, followed by your initials, for example **D1-GTW**. The database must be saved in the directory or folder called **IT Supplies**. You must also copy the file **Software** and **Invoice** to the **IT Supplies** directory or folder.

2 marks

Method

1   a   The new folder can be created using 'Windows Explorer', 'My Computer' or, if you are using an RM Connect network, the 'My Work' folder. Select File, New and Folder.

    b   Open your database program. (Remember that all the explanations illustrated in this handbook use Microsoft® Office 2000 programs. You will have slightly different procedures to follow if you are using other programs.) Select 'Blank Access database'. Select the **IT Supplies** folder and name the database according to the instructions given in the question (ie 1b).

       Copy the two text files, **Software** and **Invoice**, into this folder. From their current folder, select the two files (note, hold down the CTRL key while selecting the files so that both remain selected). Use Edit, Copy to move to the **IT Supplies** folder and Edit, Paste.

2 Use your database software to import the data file **Software** which is a comma-delimited text file containing a header row, with text data contained within quotation marks.

    a   Import this data file into a table named **Software**.

    b   During or after the import, make the first field, the **Product Number**, the primary key field.

    c   Set the data type of the **Price** and **Carriage** fields as currency with two decimal places.

    d   Introduce a validation rule for the **Carriage** field that only accepts values between £1 and £3 inclusive.

e   Use a screen dump or similar technique to show the design of the table, including the validation of the **Carriage** field. If you show the validation by entering incorrect data to display a suitable error message, make sure your printout shows both the error message and the incorrect data.

f   Place your name, today's date and the title **Printout-1** in a footer and print the table design.   **8 marks**

Method

2 a, b   To import the data file choose File, Get External Data, Import. In the Import window, select Files of type: Text Files. This will show the two text files in the folder. Select the file Software and click on the Import button. You now need to follow through the six windows of the Import Text Wizard:
1   Select Delimited.
2   Select Comma and tick the check box 'First Row contains Field Names'.
3   Select 'In a New Table'.
4   This window deals with the fields being imported. You can at this stage change the fields Price and Carriage to Currency.
5   Choose your own primary key and ensure this is the Product Number field.
6   Import to Table: Software.
(Full details of using the Import Text Wizard, with illustrations is shown on pages 92 to 94.)

c, d   In the Table Design, ensure the number of decimal places is set to two in the Price and Carriage field. In the Carriage field, enter the validation rule and text as shown in the illustration below.

Format	
Decimal Places	2
Input Mask	
Caption	
Default Value	
Validation Rule	>=1 AND <=3
Validation Text	Carriage should be between £1 and £3
Required	No
Indexed	No

Validation rule

e, f   In the Table Design view, and with the carriage field highlighted to show the validation rule, press the Print Screen (PrtSc) key on the keyboard. Open a blank Microsoft® Word document, select Edit, Paste and then add the footer, as required in question 2f.

3   A customer wants to know which Microsoft software titles are sold by
    the shop.

    a   Create a query named **Customer1** that finds all the Microsoft titles.

    b   Show only the following fields in the query and present them in the
        order **Product Number, Title, Class** and **Price.**   **6 marks**

Method

3 a, b   Select Create query in Design View. Click on the Add button to select the table
         and then Close. Select the required fields as stated in 3b. You will also need to
         select the Publisher field so that the Microsoft titles can be selected, however,
         untick the show box so that this field is not displayed when the query is run.

Untick this box so the Publisher field
does not show when the query is run

Field:	Product Number	Title	Class	Price	Publisher
Table:	Software	Software	Software	Software	Software
Sort:					
Show:	☑	☑	☑	☑	☐
Criteria:					"Microsoft"

Selects only the Microsoft titles

Customer 1 query

4   Create a report which shows the results of your query.

    a   Use the query **Customer1** to create a report in portrait form.

    b   Give the report the title **Microsoft Products.**

    c   Group your information in ascending order of **Class** and, within each
        Class, sort in ascending order of **Title.**

    d   Ensure that all the information is displayed.

    e   Place your name, today's date and the title **Printout-2** in the footer
        and print the report.   **6 marks**

Method

4a to d In the reports section, choose 'Create report by using wizard'.
        1   From the 'Tables/Queries' list box, select Query: Customer1. Select all
            the fields.

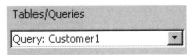

2 Select 'Class' when prompted for grouping levels.

3 For sort order, select Title, ascending order.

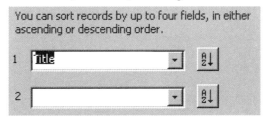

4 Select Stepped and Portrait.

5 Your choice, but Corporate is clear.

6 Title the report 'Microsoft Products'.

e In the Design View of the report, you need to add your name and the title, Printout-2. In the page footer, you will see that the Wizard has already inserted the date (as =Now()) on the left side. On the right-hand side of the page footer, delete the page number box and draw in a label box using the Label icon from the Toolbox. In the label box, enter your name and the title Printout-2. Print the report.

Label

✦ Page Footer													
=Now()											Gareth	Williams	Printout-2

Task B

5 A new customer purchases a number of software packages. Using a spreadsheet application, import the data in the text file **Invoice**.

a Import or open the text file **Invoice** into your spreadsheet.

b Adjust the column widths so that all the data is displayed.

c Save the spreadsheet using the file name **S1-** followed by your initials, for example **S1-GTW**. The spreadsheet must be saved in the directory or folder called **IT Supplies**.   **5 marks**

Method

5 a In the Microsoft® Excel spreadsheet, select File, Open. Change the 'Files of type:' to Text Files, select Invoice and click on the Open button. This will start the Import Text Wizard. Follow through three windows:

1 Ensure 'Delimited' is selected.

2 Check the 'Comma' box.

3 Select Finish.

b   The sheet now contains the invoice data, but the columns are too small to display all the details. To adjust the column widths automatically, double-click on the lines in the column header row, as shown in the illustration below.

Double-click here on the dividing line between the column headings to automatically adjust the column width

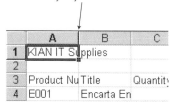

c   Because the data imported into the sheet was from a text file, it is important when saving to change the 'Save as type:' to Microsoft Excel Workbook, as shown in the illustration below.

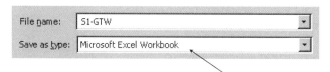

It is important to change this to 'Microsoft Excel Workbook'

6   Using the spreadsheet software, format your sheet as follows:

a   Ensure that the font used throughout the sheet is Arial (or a similar sans serif font) at size 10.

b   Increase the font size to 14 for the company name 'KIAN IT SUPPLIES' in cell A1.

c   Make the column headers in cells A3 to E3 bold text and centre the headings in the columns.

d   Underline the column headers in row 3 with a continuous line, from A3 to E3.

e   Format the cells displaying price in columns D and E to currency with two decimal places.   **6 marks**

Method

6   a   Often the default font for the sheet is Arial 10 pt but if your sheet needs changing, highlight the cells and change. **Hint:** Holding down the CTRL key and pressing A highlights the whole sheet.

b   Highlight cell A1 and increase the font size.

c, d Highlight the cells A3 to E3. Make bold and centre the text in the cell, as shown in the illustration below.

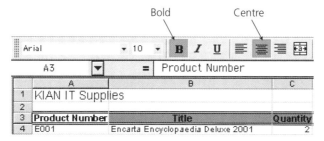

Choose Format, Cells and select the Border tab. To underline the row of cells, choose the lower line, as shown below.

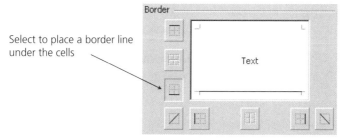

Select to place a border line under the cells

e Highlight the cells in columns D and E to be formatted (D4:E13). Choose Format, Cells and select the number tab. From the list, choose Currency and ensure it is set to display two decimal places. Take care not to format cell E1, which holds the invoice number.

7 This customer is given a 5% discount on their software purchase. Calculate the total cost as follows.

a In cell B6, show the percentage discount by inserting a 5 before the % sign.

b Use a spreadsheet formula in cells E4 to E8 to calculate the total price for each product purchased.

c Use a spreadsheet formula in cell E9 to calculate the subtotal. Place a line across the top of cell E9 to separate the subtotal.

d By using appropriate spreadsheet formulae in cells E10 to E13, calculate the 5% discount and complete the invoice to find the total amount the customer must pay. Place a line above and below the contents of cell E13.

   e   Place your name, today's date and the title **Printout-3** as a footer. Print out the spreadsheet in portrait form, ensuring that all the data is displayed on a single page.

   f   Save the sheet using the characters **S2-** followed by your initials as the file name, for example **S2-GTW**. The sheet must be saved in the directory or folder called **IT Supplies**.   **11 marks**

Method

7   a   Insert the 5 in front of the % sign in the Edit bar.

     b   In cell E4, enter the formula =C4*D4. Copy the formula down to E8.

c, d   In E9, enter the formula =sum(E4:E8) to obtain the subtotal. To insert the border line to cell E9, choose Format, Cells and select the Border tab. Place a border line at the top of the cell.
- Cell E10 shows the 5% discount of the subtotal. One formula to calculate this is =E9*5/100.
- E11 displays the new total after subtracting the discount. The formula would be =E9-E10.
- VAT (Value added tax) is 17.5% and must be calculated in cell E12. The formula is =E11*17.5/100.

The final total, displayed in cell E13, is =E11+E12. With this cell selected, choose Format, Cells and select the Border tab to place a line at the top and bottom of the cell, as shown in the illustration below.

Select to place a border line above and below the cell contents

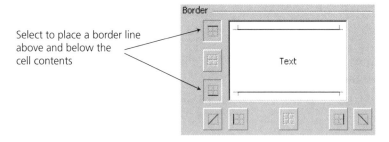

   e   To add a footer, choose File, Page Setup and select the Header/Footer tab. Click on the Custom Footer button and enter the footer details in the boxes, as shown on page 113.

Today's date can be inserted automatically

f   It is important when saving the sheet to use the 'Save As' function in the File menu. If you choose the Save icon on the toolbar, the file will be saved as S1 ... and will overwrite the earlier sheet.

8   Now print out the sheet showing the formulae in the cells as follows.

a   Change the spreadsheet display so that the formulae are displayed in the cells.

b   Change the footer title to **Printout-4** and change the paper orientation to landscape. Adjust the column widths so that all the data is displayed on one sheet of paper. Print out the sheet showing the formulae.

c   Save the sheet using the characters **S3-** followed by your initials as the file name, for example **S3-GTW**. The sheet must be saved in the directory or folder called **IT Supplies**.   **4 marks**

Method

8   a   Choose Tools, Options, then, under the View tab tick the Formulae check box.

b   Choose File, Page Setup and, under the Page tab, select the Landscape option button. Under the Header/Footer tab, change Printout-3 to Printout-4. Reduce the column widths so that the sheet fits onto one piece of paper.

c   Again, taking care not to overwrite S2-..., use the Save As command and insert the new file name.

Task C

The following task must be completed. If you have not completed this item within the allotted time, it must be carried out at the end of the test.

9   Provide a copy of all file names in the directory (folder) created during the test. This should be in the form of a screen dump showing the directory (folder) and the file names, with your name, the date and the title **Printout-5** as a footer.   **2 marks**

END OF TEST

Method

9   Using 'My Computer' (or Windows Explorer or My Work), select the IT Supplies folder where the files have been saved. (If the folder is displayed as a Web page, select View and untick the 'as Web Page' option.) Hold down the Alt key while pressing the Print Screen or PrtSc (short for print screen) key – this copies the selected screen window to the clipboard. Open a blank Microsoft® Word document and choose Edit then Paste. Choose View, Header and Footer to complete the instructions of adding your name, title and the date to the document.

The documents printed during this examination include the following:

Printout-1	Database table design and validation rule
Printout-2	Database report headed **Microsoft Products***
Printout-3	Spreadsheet showing figures*
Printout-4	Spreadsheet, landscape, showing formulae*
Printout-5	Word document, screen dump of files in the **IT Supplies** folder

* Examples of these are shown on page 115.

Printouts from the example examination paper (pages 105 to 114).

KIAN IT Supplies

| | | Invoice number | | 1245 |

Product Number	Title	Quantity	Price	Total Price
E001	Encarta Encyclopaedia Deluxe 2001	2	£38.99	£77.98
C014	Java Visual Cafe	3	£95.00	£285.00
L002	Mile Master Route Planner for Britain	1	£29.99	£29.99
C008	Video Studio 5.0	2	£59.99	£119.98
L010	Creative Art - Art Attack	4	£19.99	£79.96
			Sub Total	£592.91
	Discount 5%		Discount Due	£29.65
			Total less Discount	£563.26
			VAT @ 17.5%	£98.57
			Total	£661.84

Printout 2

	A	B	C	D	E
1	KIAN IT Supplies			Invoice number	1245
2					
3	Product Number	Title	Quantity	Price	Total Price
4	E001	Encarta Encyclopaedia Deluxe 2001	2	£38.99	£77.98
5	C014	Java Visual Cafe	3	£95.00	£285.00
6	L002	Mile Master Route Planner for Britain	1	£29.99	£29.99
7	C008	Video Studio 5.0	2	£59.99	£119.98
8	L010	Creative Art - Art Attack	4	£19.99	£79.96
9				Sub Total	£592.91
10		Discount 5%		Discount Due	£29.65
11				Total less Discount	£563.26
12				VAT @ 17.5%	£98.57
13				Total	£661.84

Printout 3

	A	B	C	D	E
1	KIAN IT Supplies			Invoice number	1245
2					
3	Product Number	Title	Quantity	Price	Total Price
4	E001	Encarta Encyclopaedia Deluxe 2001	2	38.99	=C4*D4
5	C014	Java Visual Cafe	3	95	=C5*D5
6	L002	Mile Master Route Planner for Britain	1	29.99	=C6*D6
7	C008	Video Studio 5.0	2	59.99	=C7*D7
8	L010	Creative Art - Art Attack	4	19.99	=C8*D8
9				Sub Total	=SUM(E4:E8)
10		Discount 5%		Discount Due	=E9*5/100
11				Total less Discount	=E9-E10
12				VAT @ 17.5%	=E11*0.175
13				Total	=E11+E12

Printout 4

Note, Printouts 3 and 4 of the spreadsheets on this page show both the row and column headers and grid lines. These are to help you match this sheet with your sheet on the screen. In the examination there is no requirement to print these two additional features.

Glossary

QCA/CCEA/ACCAC has provided the following glossary of terms used in Key Skills specifications.

Complex: Complex subjects and materials present a number of ideas, some of which may be abstract, very detailed or require you to deal with sensitive issues. The relationship of ideas and lines of reasoning may not be immediately clear. Specialised vocabulary and complicated sentence structures may be used.

Complex activities: The objectives or targets usually need to be agreed with others. Problems will have a number of sub-problems and will be affected by a range of factors. The tasks involved, and the relationship between them, may not be immediately clear. Situations and resources may be unfamiliar.

Complex subjects and materials: Those that include a number of ideas, some of which may be abstract, very detailed or require you to deal with sensitive issues. The relationship of ideas and lines of reasoning may not be immediately clear. Specialised vocabulary and complicated sentence structures may be used.

Critical reflection: This is taken to mean a deliberated process when you take time, within the course of your work, to focus on a period of your performance and consider carefully the thinking that led to particular actions, what happened and what you are learning from the experience, in order to inform what you might do in the future.

Dynamically complex work: Work that includes activities that are interrelated, where it is likely that action in one activity will effect changes in other aspects of the work in ways that may be difficult to predict or control (eg when external changes to timescales or resources produce new problems and you have to balance technical and human demands to meet tight deadlines).

Evidence: What you need to produce to prove you have the skills required. Examples include items you have made, written material, artwork, photographs, audio/video recordings, computer printouts of text and images, such as graphs and charts, could be used as evidence for written communication and for presenting findings in Application of Number, as well as IT. Records of problem-solving activities could include evidence of how you have worked with others, or improved you own learning and performance. Evidence can be used to back up your statements in a progress file or other record of achievement.

Extended documents: Include textbooks, reports, articles and essays of more than three pages. They may deal with straightforward or complex subjects and include images such as diagrams, pictures and charts. You are asked to read and write extended documents at Level 2 and above.

Portfolio: A file or folder for collecting and organising evidence for assessment. It should include a contents page to show where evidence for each part of the unit(s) can be found. This may be in hard copy or electronic form.

Problem: There is a problem when there is a need to bridge a gap between a current situation and a desired situation. At Levels 4 and 5, problems will be complex. They will have a number of sub-problems and will be affected by a range of factors, including a significant amount of contradictory information. They will have several possible solutions, requiring you to extend your specialist knowledge of methods and resources and adapt your strategy in working towards a satisfactory outcome.

Objectives: The purposes for working together that are shared by you and other people involved in the activity. Objectives may be those set, for example, by an organisation, your tutor, supervisor or project leader or members of your group or team.

Straightforward: Straightforward subjects and materials are those that you often meet in your work, studies or other activities. Content is put across in a direct way with the main points being easily identified. Usually, sentence structures are simple and you will be familiar with the vocabulary.

Straightforward activities: The objectives, targets or problems are given, or easily identified. It is clear how to break down the work into manageable tasks. Situations and resources are usually familiar.

Substantial activity: An activity that includes a number of related tasks, where the results of one task will affect the carrying out of the others.

Strategy: A plan, for an extended period of time, that builds on what you know from past experiences and includes the development of logical steps towards achieving a specific purpose, but also has scope to adapt approach in response to feedback from others and demands resulting from changes in the wider context of your work.

Targets: The steps for helping you to achieve your personal learning or career goals. Targets should be SMART:

- **Specific** – say exactly what you need to.
- **Measurable** – say how you will prove you have met them.
- **Achievable** – be challenging, but not too difficult for you.
- **Realistic** – have opportunities and resources for meeting them.
- **Time-bound** – include deadlines.

Useful Web sites

Key Skills Support Programme
http://www.keyskillssupport.net/

QCA Web sites

Key Skills general information
http://www.qca.org.uk/nq/ks/

Key Skills specifications
http://www.qca.org.uk/nq/ks/main2.asp

Key Skills awarding bodies
http://www.qca.org.uk/nq/ks/keyskills_ab.asp

Level 3 example tests
http://www.qca.org.uk/nq/ks/example_tests_index_3.asp

http://www.qca.org.uk/nq/ks/levels3-4/

Exam boards and awarding bodies

The following Web addresses are the specific pages in each exam board/awarding body dedicated to guidance and support for Key Skills.

AQA (Assessment and Qualifications Alliance)
http://www.aqa.org.uk/qual/keyskills.html

Edexcel
http://www.edexcel.org.uk/edexcel/subjects.nsf/(httpKeySkillsHomePage)?OpenForm

OCR (Oxford Cambridge and RSA Examinations)
http://www.ocr.org.uk/schemes/keyskills/ksindex.htm

WJEC (Welsh Joint Education Committee)
http://www.wjec.co.uk/keyskills.html

CCEA (Northern Ireland Council for the Curriculum, Examinations and Assessment)
http://www.ccea.org.uk/keyskills.htm

ASDAN (Award Scheme Development and Accreditation Network)

http://www.asdan.co.uk/

(Click on 'Key Skills' in the left-hand side menu.)

City & Guilds

http://www.key-skills.org/

Organisations

DfES (Department for Education and Skills)

http://www.dfes.gov.uk/

DfES, Key Skills

http://www.dfes.gov.uk/key/

LSC (Learning and Skills Council)

http://www.lsc.gov.uk/

UCAS (Universities and Colleges Admission Service)

http://www.ucas.ac.uk/

Resources

Key Skills Online

http://www.keyskillsonline.co.uk/

South Yorkshire Key Skills Passport

http://www.sykeyskills.co.uk/